NONPROFIT ESSENTIALS
Endowment Building

D1293879

NONPROFIT ESSENTIALS
Endowment Building

Diana S. Newman

WILEY

John Wiley & Sons, Inc.

Copyright © 2005 by John Wiley & Sons, Inc. All rights reserved.

Published by John Wiley & Sons, Inc., Hoboken, New Jersey
Published simultaneously in Canada

For general information on our other products and services, or technical support, please contact our Customer Care Department within the United States at 800-762-2974, outside the United States at 317-572-3993 or fax 317-572-4002.

Wiley also publishes its books in a variety of electronic formats. Some content that appears in print may not be available in electronic books.

Library of Congress Cataloging-in-Publication Data:

Newman, Diana S., 1943–
  Nonprofit essentials. Endowment building / Diana S. Newman.
      p. cm. — (The AFP fund development series)
  Includes index.
  ISBN 0-471-67846-5 (pbk.)
  1. Nonprofit organizations—Finance—Handbooks, manuals, etc. 2. Charities—Finance—Handbooks, manuals, etc. 3. Endowments—Handbooks, manuals, etc. 4. Deferred giving—Handbooks, manuals, etc. 5. Fund raising—Handbooks, manuals, etc. I. Title: Endowment building. II. Title. III. Series.
  HG4027.65.N48 2005
  658.15' 224—dc22
                                                          2004030073

Printed in the United States of America

10 9 8 7 6 5 4 3 2 1

This book is dedicated to my grandchildren,
Kyle, Benjamin, Rebecca, Allison, and Gregory (ages 9 to 3)
who, along with their children and their children's children—and yours—
will benefit from the charitable endowments established by our generation.

The AFP Fund Development Series

The AFP Fund Development Series is intended to provide fund development professionals and volunteers, including board members (and others interested in the not-for-profit sector), with top-quality publications that help advance philanthropy as voluntary action for the public good. Our goal is to provide practical, timely guidance and information on fundraising, charitable giving, and related subjects. AFP and Wiley each bring to this innovative collaboration unique and important resources that result in a whole greater than the sum of its parts. For information on other books in the series, please visit:

www.afpnet.org

The Association of Fundraising Professionals

The Association of Fundraising Professionals (AFP) represents 26,000 members in more than 170 chapters throughout the world, working to advance philanthropy through advocacy, research, education, and certification programs. The association fosters development and growth of fundraising professionals and promotes high ethical standards in the fundraising profession. For more information or to join the world's largest association of fundraising professionals, visit *www.afpnet.org*.

2004–2005 AFP Publishing Advisory Committee

Linda L. Chew, CFRE, Chair
Associate Director, Alta Bates Summit Foundation

Nina P. Berkheiser, CFRE
Director of Development, SPCA of Pinellas County

Samuel N. Gough, CFRE
Principal, The AFRAM Group

Robert Mueller, CFRE
Vice President, Hospice Foundation of Louisville

Maria Elena Noriega
Director, Noriega Malo & Associates

Audrey P. Kintzi, ACFRE
Chief Advancement Officer, Girl Scout Council, St. Croix Valley

D. C. Dreger, ACFRE
Senior Campaign Director, Custom Development Systems (CDS)

John Wiley & Sons

Susan McDermott
Editor (Professional/Trade Division), John Wiley & Sons

AFP Staff

Jan Alfieri
Manager, New Product Development, AFP

Walter Sczudlo
Executive Vice President, Programs and Public Policy & General Counsel

About the Author

Diana S. Newman is principal and founder of Philanthropic Resource Group, a consulting firm in Columbus, Ohio, that provides a broad range of fundraising and strategic planning services with an emphasis on planned giving and endowment building.

Before establishing Philanthropic Resource Group, Newman was Vice President for Advancement at the Columbus Foundation from 1990 to 1995. During her five-year tenure, the Columbus Foundation received gifts of $135 million, a national record for community foundations at that time. In addition, more than $250 million in planned gifts from 210 families were documented. From 1983 to 1990, Newman was the founding director of the Ohio Historical Foundation, the fundraising arm of the Ohio Historical Society.

In 2002, Newman authored *Opening Doors: Pathways to Diverse Donors*, published by Jossey-Bass and the winner of the 2003 AFP/Skystone Ryan Prize for Research. She is also a contributing author of *Cultures of Caring: Philanthropy in Diverse American Communities*, published in 1999 by the Council on Foundations and funded by the Ford, Kellogg, and Packard foundations. In addition, she wrote *Community Foundation Fundamentals* (2001) and *Resource Development for Community Foundations* (2002), faculty and student course guides for staff and board members sponsored by the Community Foundations

Institute, a joint project of the Council on Foundations in Washington, D.C., and Indiana University's Center on Philanthropy. Newman is a member of the National Board of Gift-Planning Consultants for *Planned Giving Mentor*, a newsletter for newcomers to gift planning published in Edmonds, Washington.

A frequent speaker, teacher, and facilitator at conferences across the country and abroad, Newman has given presentations for the American Red Cross, YMCA of North America, Alzheimer's Association, National Committee on Planned Giving, Council on Foundations, Association of Fundraising Professionals, Canadian Association of Gift Planners, National Conference on Black Philanthropy, and The Foundation Center. She was the keynote speaker at a philanthropy conference in Seoul, Korea, sponsored by the Beautiful Foundation in November 2003. Currently, Newman is working with the Ohio Arts Council on a project to assist three Chilean arts organizations headquartered in Santiago.

Newman is the cofounder of the original *Leave A Legacy* program in Columbus, a community-wide collaboration to encourage people from all walks of life to leave gifts to the charities of their choice. *Leave A Legacy* is now a North American program sponsored by the National Committee on Planned Giving in more than 70 communities in the United States and 21 in Canada.

Newman was president of the Central Ohio Planned Giving Council and served on the board of directors for the National Committee on Planned Giving. She is currently on the board of the Central Ohio Chapter of the Association of Fundraising Professionals, which named her as its 2004 Outstanding Fundraising Professional, and serves on AFP's International Research Council.

Her husband, Dennis, is an attorney. They have three children and five grandchildren.

Contents

Contents

Foreword

The end of the twentieth century has been characterized by historians as a period of unprecedented economic growth. Philanthropic support across the board enjoyed new and higher levels of success. The growth in the financial markets of the 1990s decade provided the opportunity for charitable organizations not only to rejuvenate long-standing core programs, but also to initiate new and exciting ventures previously constrained by budgetary restrictions. As the century came to a close, charitable organizations were setting and achieving new fundraising records.

The beginning of the twenty-first century ushered in a dramatically different economic landscape. The "irrational exuberance" of soaring markets came to an abrupt halt as the broader financial markets "corrected." Significant individual and corporate fortunes were lost virtually over night. The ripple effect was felt not only on personal and business levels, but throughout the third sector as pledge commitments and contributions fell. Hardest hit were those charitable organizations with little or no reserves to support increasing financial strains on the operating budget. For many organizations, it was, and continues to be, their endowment that has made the difference between sustained financial viability and painful hardship.

Endowment income provides critical long-term financial stability to support the people and programs that our charities serve. Indeed, the Harvard University endowment, valued at over $23 billion at the end of fiscal year 2004, is a collection of more than 10,500 separate funds established over the years to provide financial assistance to deserving students; to maintain its libraries, museums, and collections; to support teaching and research activities; and to provide ongoing support for a wide variety of other programs and activities. These funds together generate almost 30 percent of Harvard's annual operating budget.

All of these separately endowed funds have one objective: to support initiatives not for just one year, or even one generation, but in perpetuity. Indeed, one of Harvard's earliest endowed funds was established in 1643 by way of a gift of one hundred pounds from Lady Ann Mowlson to provide a stipend for scholarships. Over 360 years later, her endowed fund continues to provide valuable support to some of the almost 70 percent of the Harvard undergraduates who receive financial assistance.

Equally as important as the use to which endowment income is applied, it is incumbent on charitable organizations to manage their endowments so that the purchasing power of the principal is protected from market downturns and from the corrosive effects of inflation. If charities are successful in doing this, endowment distributions will likely retain their value and impact for years, generations, and centuries.

Author Diana S. Newman, principal of Philanthropic Resources Group, is well qualified to identify and address the challenges of starting and building an endowment. I first met Diana when our paths crossed as volunteer board members of a national planned giving organization. Her extensive background in offering strategic planning, evaluation, and fundraising services for community foundations and other nonprofit organizations has served her well in meeting the challenges of writing about this important topic. Diana's useful

"Tips & Techniques" and "In the Real World" are especially helpful in placing theory in a context of practice.

This book is the most comprehensive and thoughtfully presented guide I have read on building endowments. I believe it will be especially beneficial to fundraisers in small and mid-sized organizations who have been charged with building an endowment on top of a myriad of other responsibilities. Experienced fundraisers, planned giving officers, CEOs, and volunteer leadership of nonprofit organizations who are reinvigorating or expanding an endowment-building effort will also find *Nonprofit Essentials: Endowment Building* an extremely valuable resource.

The case for initiating or expanding an endowment has never been more compelling. It is estimated that at least $41 trillion will pass from one generation to the next by the year 2052. As endowments enrich the missions of the organizations we serve, Diana's significant contribution will enrich our understanding of the importance and magnitude of the work that lies ahead.

Peter K. Kimball
Director of Gift Planning
Harvard University

Preface

In my first job as a professional fundraiser, I was charged with increasing net receipts from annual gifts, running a membership program, managing a 200-person volunteer corps, overseeing fundraising and recognition events, developing a capital campaign program, and writing grant proposals. And, oh yes, establishing an endowment.

As the sole member of the development staff—and even when the staff grew to seven professionals—I never got around to building the endowment because other tasks always took precedence, and I was not sure how endowments actually worked. How could I spend time building long-term relationships when there were so many other more pressing demands on my time? Why would donors give their hard-earned money to endowment, rather than to provide tangible help immediately? How could I justify working on gifts that might not be realized for years? Wouldn't a large endowment—if we had one—encourage donors to slack off on their annual giving? Where could I turn to learn about this seemingly complex topic, and what should I do first?

Nonprofit Essentials: Endowment Building is written to begin to answer these and many more questions about endowments that development officers ask. It is the book I wish I had had as I started my fundraising career. Instead,

I learned most of what I know about endowment building from experienced mentors, patient donors, planned giving seminars, experimentation with many strategies and tactics—and my mistakes. I hope the reader will have a shorter learning curve than I have had.

Purpose

This is a practical guide in an easily digestible format for staff and board members of charitable organizations in the United States. It provides the background needed to assess whether and when to start an endowment building effort. It offers guidance to develop an Endowment Action Program appropriate to the needs and resources of each nonprofit organization. It suggests strategies to successfully establish and grow charitable endowments. Yet it is more than a how-to book; it is a how-to-think-about book. Although *Nonprofit Essentials: Endowment Building* contains many concrete suggestions, it also stretches the reader to think more broadly and deeply about discovering donors' values and helping them achieve their philanthropic dreams.

Audience

Development professionals who have recently been assigned to either start or grow an endowment fund are the primary audience for this book. They may be employed by an established organization with a large development staff or by a small grassroots organization with a volunteer-led development effort. The principles of endowment building are the same, although the scope of the programs will vary.

Although *Nonprofit Essentials: Endowment Building* is written with the expectation that its readers already have development experience, those who are new to fundraising will benefit from this book as well. Many inexperienced fundraisers are in small and midsized organizations and have been asked to build an endowment while also raising current funds and tending to many other fundraising tasks, as I was in my first job. These "newbies" will find basic information and encouragement in the chapters that follow to begin an effective, long-term endowment building program that will not overwhelm them or their organization.

Other people will find value in this book as well: executive directors and board members of nonprofit organizations that are considering beginning an endowment building effort; development officers who want to incorporate new endowment building programs into existing development efforts; and experienced planned giving or development officers in charge of building endowments who want to solve particular problems, look for examples of proven practices, or refresh their endowment building skills. Endowment fundraisers who want validation for their recommendations to the executive director or board members will find that support here.

Readers' Return on Investment

After completing this book, readers will be able to:

- Assess the organization's readiness and commitment to building an endowment.

- Describe the pros and cons of proactively seeking contributions for the organizations' endowment funds.

- Use a working vocabulary applicable to the endowment building field.

- Develop and carry out an Endowment Action Program appropriate to the organization.

- Identify, cultivate, and solicit prospective donors to the endowment.

- Establish critically important policies and procedures.

- Understand and discuss the issues related to management and investment of the assets.

- Provide appreciation to and recognition of donors for their support and commitment.

- Work with allied professionals to help donors achieve their charitable goals.

- Market the endowment to likely prospective donors and their professional advisors.

- Measure the success of the endowment building program and share meaningful data with the board and other stakeholders.

Overview of the Content

Chapter 1, Understanding Endowment, serves as an introduction to the book by describing the value of the endowment to the organization, the donor, and the fundraiser. It defines the three kinds of endowments and the importance of understanding the vocabulary of endowment. A primer on the kinds of gifts available to donors is included, intended to demystify the technical terms associated with endowment building and planned giving. A brief history of endowment points out that endowments have helped provide charitable services since the Roman Empire—and are becoming increasingly important to nonprofit organizations today.

Chapter 2, Preplanning and Assessing Readiness for Endowment, begins by describing the prime factors in successful endowment programs and the kinds of organizations that should not establish endowments. It discusses the training and experience needed by development officers for endowment building work and the process to assess an organization's readiness to undertake a program to establish or increase its endowment. It also describes the importance of identifying endowment champions and engaging volunteers.

Chapter 3, Developing the Case for Support and the Endowment Action Program, sets forth the importance of a written program, of enthusiastic support from the board of directors, and of a compelling case for endowment support.

It describes options for the structure of the endowment fundraising program, staffing and budget considerations, and development of the Endowment Action Program.

Chapter 4, Identifying, Cultivating, and Soliciting Prospective Donors, describes how to identify qualified prospective donors and the values and motivations that may lead them to make endowment gifts. The importance of wealth, age, family circumstances, giving history, and race and ethnicity are discussed. This chapter lists the pros and cons of various strategies to cultivate prospective donors, emphasizing the critical importance of personal, face-to-face visits with prospective donors by staff and volunteers. In addition, it presents techniques to close gifts and ways to follow up with donors after gifts are completed.

Chapter 5, Managing, Investing, and Establishing Policies, lays out options for the important task of managing and investing the assets of the endowment and monitoring investment performance. It also offers concrete suggestions for developing a comprehensive Endowment Policy Manual, with examples in the Appendix.

Chapter 6, Caring for Donors and the People They Trust, offers practical tips for responding to inquiries from prospective donors, acknowledging gifts, and recognizing donors. It discusses donor stewardship issues and demonstrates ways to encourage contributions from specific groups of donors and to work with family members and professional advisors.

Chapter 7, Marketing the Endowment, focuses on communicating the endowment's case for support to various market segments. It describes the advantages (and disadvantages) of particular marketing strategies and tools, and lists considerations for selecting the most appropriate strategy for a particular group of prospective donors. It also lays out compelling themes and messages about the endowment.

Chapter 8, Measuring Success, concludes the book by describing ways to measure and report the activities undertaken to generate gifts to the endowment and the results of those activities. It offers a format to report the endowment's revenue, investment results, projections, and confirmed expectancies. In addition, it describes measurements of performance, which are especially important to review annually, because gifts may not actually be received for years.

At the end of the book are the Appendixes, containing useful documents and materials referred to in the text; the Glossary, a compilation of words defined throughout the book as well as the most common terms used in endowment building literature; and the References, a list of publications used in its preparation. An Index is included as well.

How to Use This Book

Readers who are new to the field of endowment building will receive the most benefit from the book by reading it in sequential order, from cover to cover. Board members and CEOs of nonprofit organizations that are considering beginning an endowment building program will find Chapters 1, 2, and 8 to be particularly helpful. Planned giving and development officers who want to solve particular problems with their endowment building efforts may want to look in the Index for specific issues or examples of proven practices. This book can also be used as a refresher course for those who have been involved with endowment building for a long time and want to update their skills.

Throughout *Nonprofit Essentials: Endowment Building*, the reader will find that "In the Real World" sections provide practical examples of how nonprofit organizations have addressed specific issues. "Tips & Techniques" sections offer guidance on how to handle specific situations and concrete steps to solve particular problems.

Acknowledgments

I am indebted to family, friends, colleagues, and clients for the wide variety of gifts they have bestowed on me: permitting me to work with them in achieving their charitable goals; collaborating with me in growing endowment funds for organizations; demonstrating effective tactics and skills while we worked together shoulder-to-shoulder, and sharing stories, insights, and experiences that have influenced and enriched my own endowment building efforts.

I especially thank three colleagues in Columbus who read early drafts of this manuscript and offered valuable advice for improvements and clarifications: Doug Allinger, founder of Allinger and Company, Inc.; Laura MacDonald, president of Benefactors Counsel; and Mike O'Sullivan, senior vice president for development at Children's Hospital Foundation. I'm also grateful to Susan Axelrod, a colleague on the National Board of Gift Planning Consultants for *Planned Giving Mentor*, for tackling the job of collecting stories for the "In the Real World" sections of the book.

I met Peter Kimball, director of gift planning at Harvard University, through our joint service on the board of the National Committee on Planned Giving. He graciously accepted my invitation to write a Foreword to the book. Thank you, Peter.

My last and most heartfelt acknowledgment is reserved for my husband of 40 years, Dennis, who supported me throughout the process of developing this book with his red pen, great cooking, and incomparable back rubs.

Disclaimer

I am not an accountant, attorney, financial planner, insurance professional, investment broker, or realtor. I am a fundraiser. Nothing in *Nonprofit Essentials: Endowment Building* should be construed as legal or financial advice. Please review legal or financial matters with qualified professionals.

The Shift to Endowment Building

Development officers who have recently moved into endowment building often need to adjust their mindsets, shift their thinking. They may have been accustomed to working with annual donors, who are often motivated to make a $100 gift because of the needs of the organization or its clients. They may be used to major gift donors, who may make a $10,000 gift because of interest in a particular program, the opportunity to see their names on a plaque, or peer pressure. The $1 million endowment donors, however, are primarily concerned with what they want to accomplish in their lives and with the legacies they will leave to the community.

Jim Gillespie, with CommonWealth Consultants in Indianapolis, says that moving from being an annual fund development officer to being an endowment gift officer is like moving from selling Saturn sedans to Lamborghinis—the development officer is not selling transportation any more. In fact, the development officer is not selling at all. He or she is helping people fund their dreams and perpetuate their values.

Those who are successful in endowment building understand the differences in this kind of fundraising. The skills needed in the annual fund office are not necessarily transferable to endowment building; new skills are needed. *Nonprofit Essentials: Endowment Building* will help development officers, and others involved in the endowment building process, acquire and become comfortable with these new skills and new ways to approach their work.

CHAPTER 1

Understanding Endowment

After reading this chapter, you will be able to

- Define the three types of endowments.
- List the benefits of endowments for the organization, its donors, and its fundraising staff.
- Describe how endowment building and planned giving work together.
- Understand kinds of endowment gifts and gift vehicles—and their benefits.
- Review the history of endowments from ancient times to the present.

Life is not a "brief candle." It is a splendid torch that I want to make burn as brightly as possible before handing it on to future generations.

—George Bernard Shaw

What is the use of living, if it not be to strive for noble causes and
to make this muddled world a better place for those who will live
in it after we are gone?

—Sir Winston Churchill

Endowments are hot topics these days. In nearly every issue, *The Chronicle of Philanthropy*[1] describes multimillion-dollar gifts to the endowments of some of the largest and most powerful charitable organizations, especially universities and hospital systems. But many organizations are not included in this outpouring of largess. And often the executive directors and board members of nonprofit organizations are confused about the hoopla about endowments. Unfortunately, these leaders do not perceive that endowment building is possible— or even desirable—for *their* organizations.

Many small and midsized nonprofit organizations—colleges, hospitals and health centers, social service agencies, arts and cultural organizations, community foundations, secondary schools, religious congregations, neighborhood associations, and so forth—have no or very small endowments. These organizations have lived through decreases in federal, state, and local governmental support for many core programs. They have experienced the loss of grant opportunities from private and corporate foundations, receding support from local corporations that have been purchased by out-of-town interests, disappearing or nonexistent reserve funds, market declines, and exhausted, overburdened, and increasingly selective individual donors. These are the organizations to which this book is directed.

The decreasing revenue sources and rising expenses incurred by nonprofit organizations make endowment distributions an increasingly crucial funding element. Organizations that have relied heavily on one or two sources of charitable support have been particularly vulnerable to the uncertainties of the economy, the vagaries of the stock market, and the instability of other funding sources. They may be ripe to establish or reinvigorate an endowment building program.

Endowments, generally, are funds containing financial assets that are held permanently by nonprofit organizations and invested to generate income and capital appreciation for the benefit of the organization. A reasonable portion of the endowment's value is spent annually to support the organization and its purposes, while the excess income and/or appreciation are accumulated in the fund so that it grows, over time. Endowments can be established to support the ongoing operating expenses of the organization or for designated purposes such as scholarships, projects, programs, institutes, professorships, or any aspect of its charitable work.

Although an endowment is not the panacea that many boards of directors hope for, it can offer ongoing operating funds and welcome sources of revenue when money is tight, as well as a wellspring of resources for new programs and innovations in prosperous years.

This chapter lists the benefits of endowments for the organization, its donors, and its fundraising staff. It describes the three primary kinds of endowments, how endowment building and planned giving work together, and the various kinds and timing of endowment gifts. It ends by putting the concept of endowment in an historical context.

The Benefits of an Endowment

Endowments offer benefits to the organization, to the donor, and to the fundraiser.

To the Organization

There are advantages of a significant and growing endowment to the board of directors, CEO, officers, fundraisers, and staff members of the nonprofit organization. Here is a list of at least some of the benefits:

- *Creates an ongoing source of income.* Because a permanent endowment is an invested pool of money that provides a reliable source of income in perpetuity, the organization can count on annual distributions for its charitable work. Funds may be designated for endowment by the donor or by the board of directors. With appropriate investment and spending policies, discussed in Chapter 5, the endowment's purchasing power will be preserved. Thus, a fund that generates income to operate a reading recovery program for elementary students today can be designed to produce income to run the same program 20 years from now and beyond. The endowment also grows over time with additional gifts from multiple donors.

- *Enhances stability and prestige.* A well-managed endowment sends a message of planned long-term stability, fiscal responsibility, and financial viability. It enhances the organization's prestige and credibility.

- *Relieves pressure on the annual fund.* Annual fund goals tend to rise right along with the cost of providing services and operating the organization, but the ability of the annual fund to meet increasing demand is not limitless. An endowment can provide annual support for the organization's operating budget.

- *Allows program expansion.* Program expansion can be funded with distributions from endowment funds used for scholarships, faculty chairs, staff positions, lecture series, research, facility maintenance, equipment and supplies, and for any other purpose designated by the donor or by the board of directors.

- *Provides independence.* Endowment contributions designated for specific purposes can provide a measure of independence from economic, governmental, and political forces. For example, an Indiana retirement community was in danger of losing its chaplain when the board resolved to terminate all programs except those that generated enough income to be self-sustaining. The chaplaincy program survived, however, after a concerned donor made a gift of endowment funds that were sufficient to support the program. The program continues and also enjoys a measure of independence from the need to generate income to support itself.

- *Offers flexibility for management.* Endowments offer options to meet new challenges by providing greater financial flexibility and self-sustaining income streams. Endowments can augment uncertain income sources, broaden the overall revenue mix, improve the income statement, and provide leverage for bond-rating capacity and loans for new facilities.

- *Builds pipeline of future gifts.* A growing endowment builds a pipeline of gifts that will mature in the future, because many endowment gifts are designed to be used at a future date, often upon the death of the donor. An organization that attracts deferred gifts enhances its future financial security and positions itself to enjoy increasingly larger gifts in the future.

- *Encourages outright gifts.* Outright gifts as well as other kinds of planned gifts are encouraged by building an endowment. Donors who have decided to make an endowment gift to the organization are likely to make gifts to the organization's annual and capital campaigns as well. After all, they have already made a commitment to the organization's future.

To the Donor

Endowment contributions—both those that create new funds and those that add to existing funds—provide numerous benefits to donors, which the development staff must understand and be able to articulate to prospective contributors and to their financial and legal advisors.

- *Perpetuates the donor's values and priorities.* An endowment gift can perpetuate the donor's values in the wake of change; it can provide assurance that programs that are important to the donor will survive. By creating or adding to a permanent endowment for a designated purpose, the donor seeks to enable and obligate the organization to carry out his or her expressed wishes, so long as it is practical and possible to do so. A restricted endowment can ensure organizational support for the donor's priorities.

For example, the Indiana donor who established the chaplaincy endowment at the retirement community did so because he valued the chaplain's services during his wife's stay at the center, and he wanted to ensure that the program would continue even during budget crises at present or in the future.

- *Creates a sense of immortality.* Because an endowment gift will be invested permanently, it can serve as a permanent tribute to the donor and extend the donor's values for future generations. It can offer the donor a sense of immortality, a way to define the donor's place in the cosmic scheme of things through support of an important cause.

- *Makes significant investment in the future.* Many donors make larger endowment gifts, often through planned giving vehicles, than they dreamed were possible. Endowment gifts are sometimes the donor's last (and largest) gift to the organizations they value most. Donors can receive great satisfaction from making a significant contribution from assets accumulated over their lifetimes. In the case of deferred planned gifts, the gifts may be the donors' final acts of contributing to the organization or the work that they find most valuable.

- *Endows annual gifts.* An endowment gift gives donors the option to perpetuate their annual gifts. For example, the $100 per year donor might make a $2,000 endowment gift in order to continue annual gifts of $100 to the organization in the future. This concept is often appealing to the consistent older donor. For example, an 82-year-old woman who had given $1,200 to her local chapter of the Multiple Sclerosis Society each year since her husband was diagnosed with multiple sclerosis 15 years earlier found comfort in creating a $25,000 deferred endowment, which, at 5%, generated the same $1,200 annually for the Society following her death.

- *Allows incremental funding.* Some donors do not want to give away their assets during their lifetimes, yet they want to see the benefits of the gift immediately. They establish endowment gifts through bequests or other gift vehicles that take place after their lifetimes. Then they make gifts annually that represent the amount that would have been distributed from the endowment if their gift had already been received. In this way, their annual gifts can provide the support currently that their planned gift will provide eventually.

- *Provides lifetime income.* Some kinds of endowment gifts—split interest gifts—pay income to the donor for life, with the remainder going to the charity's endowment after the donor's death. These kinds of gifts, discussed in more detail in the next section, can provide stable income to the donor during retirement or can help the donor meet family obligations.

- *Alleviates management burden.* Some donors, particularly as they become older, are uneasy with managing their assets and making investment decisions. A split interest gift enables the donor to receive regular income for life without the burden or cost of managing investments.

- *Permits additions at a later time.* An endowment fund can be added to later. The donor, or the donor's friends and family, can add to a named fund from time to time by simply identifying the fund as the object of the gift. It makes a handy vehicle for people, especially family members, who wish to make meaningful gifts to people who already have enough "stuff."

To the Fundraiser

The fundraising professional who is charged with overseeing the growth of the endowment—and all other fundraisers on the staff—must understand the advantages of a large and growing endowment from their standpoint if they are to make endowment building a priority.

- *Protects against ever-increasing annual fund goals.* Endowments can protect against unreasonable, ever-increasing annual fund goals. Many organizations attempt to balance their budgets by increasing annual fund goals, even when the goals are not realistic or attainable. A significant endowment offers the opportunity to mitigate difficult economic circumstances and even out the organization's inclination to focus solely on short-term annual fundraising goals.

- *Offers options to donors.* Increasingly, sophisticated donors expect endowments as an option. Fundraisers want and need to have a full array of giving opportunities to offer donors. Endowments are attractive for all of the reasons described previously and, often, because they do not have as much pressure of immediacy that exists with annual or capital gifts.

- *Devotes resources toward it.* Once endowment building is institutionalized, the organization's resources—staff, board, money, time—are consistently devoted to it. Fundraisers at organizations committed to growing endowments spend at least a portion of their time with prospective endowment donors and talk about the endowment routinely with all prospective donors. Small and midsized organizations may have limited staff and other resources, but they can still carry out a strategic endowment program, even if it is scaled back. Organizations with large staffs make endowment building the full-time responsibility of one or more staff members. The development program, regardless of the size of the organization, balances its efforts to bring in dollars today while building an endowment for the future. Fundraising professionals spend time growing the endowment and are measured appropriately for their efforts, as discussed in more detail in Chapter 8.

- *Attracts new donors.* Endowments often tap new and different donors for support. These donors focus on gifts of assets rather than cash, and gifts from net worth rather than cash flow. Because of their opportunity for long-term and future focus, endowments attract committed visionaries. After endowment donors have made their commitments, they often become consistent annual donors as well, because they have made significant commitments to the organization's future.

- *Focuses on the donor's objectives.* Endowment fundraising demands a donor-centered focus. Endowment fundraising helps leadership and fundraising staff members remember that the donor is in control of the gift. The donor's money and the donor's dream drive the gift. The donor determines the size and form of the gift. The donor determines the timing of the gift. The organization must be prepared to focus on meeting the donor's intellectual, psychological, and financial needs. Even though the organization may want unrestricted current contributions, the donor's wishes trump the organization's needs every time. The organization must be willing to be as visionary as the donor, perhaps taking risks in programmatic and financial areas.

Definitions to Keep in Mind

Several words and concepts need to be understood before delving more deeply into building endowments.

Endowment

An *endowment* is a broad term that is often used to describe the total of one or more endowed funds. An endowed fund is a charitable gift established in perpetuity in which the principal is invested for total return (both income and appreciation) and a small portion of the fund's balance (usually 4 to 6%) is paid out, generally on an annual basis. The *beginning principal* is the value of the asset that was contributed by the donor; the **income** is the earnings produced by the principal; and *appreciation* (or *depreciation*) is the gain (or loss) in the value of the principal since it was contributed. An organization may have several endowed funds, established by one or more donors and for one or more purposes, in its endowment.

Merriam-Webster's Collegiate Dictionary, 10th Edition, states that to endow is "to furnish with an income for the continuing support or maintenance of an organization." An endowment, then, is simply a pool of money that is invested to provide ongoing financial resources for the organization's operations or for specific programs. Both state laws and accounting board standards apply to endowments.

The Uniform Management of Institutional Funds Act (UMIFA) governs endowment spending by charitable corporations and by some trusts. All states, except Alaska, Pennsylvania, and South Dakota, have enacted some form of this law since it was first approved in 1972. A copy of the Act is included in Appendix A. It is written with a minimum of legalese, and development and finance staff members should read it.

In *Building an Endowment Right from the Start*, Lynda Moerschbaecher says: "In states where a state adopts the model or uniform law, each state has the right to select or reject provisions, to modify those provision or to adopt the law in whole. Therefore, every organization must check its own state law to learn the nonprofit corporate code or UMIFA rules adopted by that particular state."[2]

Janne G. Gallagher, senior counsel for the Council on Foundations, says:

> Before UMIFA, charity managers often believed that they could not rely on outside experts for investment advice and that investments had to be limited to the safest possible vehicles—cash, government bonds and, perhaps, a few blue chip stocks. UMIFA not only freed charity managers to delegate investment decisions to outside managers, but also allowed them to invest assets for long-term growth, not just current yields. . . . Because UMIFA lets charity managers invest for growth, not just income, UMIFA also allows them to take that growth into account in making spending decisions for endowed funds.[3]

The UMIFA defines an *endowment fund* as "an institutional fund, or any part thereof, not wholly expendable on a current basis under the terms of the donor's gift agreement."[4]

The Financial Accounting Standards Board (FASB) has identified three types of endowments:

1. *True endowment* (also called Permanent Endowment). The UMIFA definition of endowment describes true endowment in most states. In these cases, the *donor* has stated that the gift is to be held permanently as an endowment, either for general purposes or for specific programs as identified in a written gift agreement. True endowment is restricted in a written agreement by the donor or is in response to a solicitation that promised to use the gift as an endowment. Under FASB, the portion of the permanent endowment that must be maintained permanently (not used up, expended, or otherwise exhausted) is classified as *permanently restricted net assets.*

2. *Quasi-endowment* (also known as Funds Functioning as Endowment—FFE). Reserve funds, financial windfalls, or unrestricted gifts that the board elects to put into endowment are quasi-endowments. Because a future board could vote to remove part or all of the quasi-endowment's principal, it is not a true endowment. A board-designated endowment is classified as *unrestricted net assets,* and its principal may be spent under FASB guidelines. Thus, if the board established an endowed fund, it is quasi-endowment. If the donor makes a gift for an endowed fund, it is true endowment.

3. *Term endowment.* An endowment created for a set period of years or until a future event (such as the death of the donor) is known as a term endowment. After the term runs out or the event takes place, the principal may be expended. The portion of the term endowment that must be maintained for the specific term is classified by the FASB as *temporarily restricted net assets.*

The endowed funds in the organization's endowment must be clearly labeled as one of these three types for accounting purposes. Each of these types may be used for designated or undesignated gifts—for general purposes or to benefit specific projects such as scholarships, professorships, camperships, staff positions, trainings, lecture series, and innovative programs.

Endowment Program

An endowment program is an integral part of an organization's comprehensive development program. It is a planned, consistent, and unending effort to build permanent endowment funds to support the work of the organization. Because endowments typically build slowly, primarily based on long-standing relationships between the donor and the organization and its leadership, endowment programs should be established by organizations that are committed to the growth of the endowment and comfortable with the long-term nature of endowment building.

The Role of Endowment in Planned Giving

Planned Giving

Planned giving, or gift planning as it is sometimes called, is the preparation and design of charitable gifts to maximize benefits for both the donor and the organization. The Association of Fundraising Professionals defines planned giving as "the integration of sound personal, financial and estate planning concepts with the individual donor's plan for lifetime and testamentary giving."[5] Paul Schervish, director of the Center on Wealth and Philanthropy at Boston College, defines a planned gift as "any gift that combines conscientious decisions about how much to give, to whom to give it, and when to give it. As such, virtually all giving, from all people, at all times is planned giving."[6] Planned giving is the process of choosing the most appropriate gift for the most important purpose in the most advantageous time frame for the donor, the charity, and the donor's heirs.

Planned gifts, both current and deferred, can be completely unrestricted or directed to capital campaigns, specific projects, annual funds, or endowments. They are often given from accumulated assets, rather than current earnings. They are usually larger than operating fund gifts and completed infrequently, rather than annually.

Endowments

Endowment building is different from planned giving. The endowment is what you do with the gift, rather than the planning for the gift or the gift itself. A true endowment gift is permanently invested, not spent for current operations or capital projects. It is held by the organization in perpetuity, with a portion of the endowment's value used annually as the donor requested. Frank Minton, with Planned Giving Services in Seattle, Washington, states: "Most endowments have been built by planned gifts. Planned gifts and endowment gifts should therefore work in tandem."[7]

Kinds of Gifts Available to Donors

Endowments can be established with gifts now. They can also be created in the future through a will or trust, and a wide variety of planned gifts are available to create endowments. Although it is beyond the scope of this book to detail the technicalities and specifics of various kinds of gift options, it is important that fundraisers understand the basic concepts and benefits behind gift options.

Charitable gifts can be divided into three categories: (1) immediate or outright gifts, (2) deferred gifts, and (3) deferred gifts with income benefits.

Immediate or Outright Gifts

Outright gifts to endowment funds permit the immediate long-term investment of the gift to provide support either for purposes designated by the donor or, if the donor has made no designation, for purposes chosen by the board of directors. These gifts are most desirable to the organization, because they provide immediate funds or assets that can be invested now to provide ongoing revenue for the organization.

- *Cash.* The most familiar type of gift is cash, usually given through a check written by the donor. Nonprofit organizations are pleased to accept checks in any amount, although most require a minimum-size

TIPS & TECHNIQUES

IRS Resources to Keep
in the Office

The Internal Revenue Service (IRS) offers several valuable documents through its Web site. Publication 526, "Charitable Contributions," describes contributions that donors can and cannot deduct from federal income taxes, contributions of real estate and personal property, limits on deductions, and other useful information. It can be found at *www.irs.gov/pub/irs-pdf/p526.pdf*.

The IRS publishes a document to help determine the value of charitable gifts (Publication 561, "Determining the Value of Donated Property," *www.irs.gov/pub/irs-pdf/p561.pdf*). The Publication is designed to help donors and appraisers determine the value of property (other than cash) that is given to qualified charities. It also explains what kind of information the donor needs to provide to support the charitable contribution deduction claimed on the donor's tax return.

Publication 1771, "Charitable Contributions—Substantiation and Disclosure Requirements," explains the federal tax law for charitable organizations that receive tax-deductible charitable contributions and for taxpayers who make contributions. It details the requirements for written acknowledgments, defines the goods or services that organizations may provide for contributions, and describes requirements for unreimbursed expenses—with many useful examples. It can be downloaded from *www.irs.gov/pub/irs-pdf/p1771.pdf*.

The reporting and taxation of gains (or losses) of appreciated property— stocks, bonds, real estate, real property—are described in Publication 17, Reporting Gains and Losses, available at *www.irs.gov/publications/ p17/ch17.html#d0e43615*.

Form 8283 (and instructions) is available at the IRS Web site at *www.irs. gov/pub/irs-pdf/f8283.pdf*. Every donor of noncash contributions to a charitable organization that exceed a certain amount must file Form gift to establish a named endowment fund. Donors need to be reminded to note on the check or in the accompanying letter that the gift is for the endowment—either the general endowment or a specifically named endowed fund.

Outright gifts of cash are fully deductible for federal income-tax purposes up to 50% of adjusted gross income. If the donor's total gifts exceed 50% of adjusted gross income, the excess may be carried forward for tax purposes for up to five additional years.

- *Stocks and bonds.* Nonprofits accept gifts of publicly traded stocks and bonds at fair-market value. Fair-market value is determined under IRS rules. Generally, gifts of publicly traded securities are sold by the organization as soon as possible, and the proceeds from the sale are added to the appropriate endowed fund, after commissions and expenses, if any. Nonprofit organizations also accept gifts of shares of mutual funds.

A gift of appreciated stock held by a donor for more than a year offers the donor a three-fold tax savings. First, the donor avoids paying any long-term capital gains tax on the increase in value of the stock. Second, the donor receives an income tax deduction for the full fair-market value of the stock on the date of the gift. For income tax purposes, the fair-market value of such gifts is deductible up to 30% of adjusted gross income, with an additional five-year carry forward. Finally, because it has been given to charity, the stock will not be subject to estate tax upon the donor's death.

Both publicly traded securities and closely held stock can be used as gift assets, although many smaller organizations may want to stay clear of closely held stock because of the possibility that it may cost more to administer than the net value of the gift to the organization. If closely held stock is offered as a gift, both the donor and the organization should obtain professional advice. A local community foundation may be able to assist the organization in completing such a gift.

- ○ *Publicly traded securities.* For publicly traded securities—those on the public markets such as the New York Stock Exchange or NASDAQ—the value of the gift is the average of the high and the low price of the stock on the day the gift is complete. This is an important concept and a calculation that is more complex than you might expect. (See Tips & Techniques, IRS Resources to Keep in the Office, "Determining the Value of Donated Property.")

- ○ *Closely held stock.* For closely held stock—stock that is not publicly traded, such as family businesses—value is determined by an independent appraiser, usually paid for by the donor. This is significantly more complex than publicly traded stock, where the value can be easily determined. Proposed gifts of closely held stock and partnership interests should be reviewed and approved both by the organization's legal counsel and by the board of directors.

- • *Real estate.* Gifts of real estate should be reviewed and approved by the organization's board of directors. Donors should be required to provide evidence of clear title to the property and Phase I environmental assessments as well as legal descriptions of the property. Donors will need independent appraisals to submit with their tax returns. Before acceptance of a gift of real estate, the organization and the donor should agree, in writing, on arrangements for paying the expenses associated with the property, including taxes and assessments, insurance coverage, and maintenance costs. The organization should review any liabilities, restrictions, or other conditions related to the gift. The organization should establish clear policies that apply to its acceptance of gifts of real estate in order to cover all of the issues peculiar to real estate and gifts of entities with assets that include real estate. (See the discussion of Acceptance Policies for Endowment Gifts in the section on Developing an Endowment Policy Manual in Chapter 5.)

When an individual makes an outright gift of real estate to an organization, the donor can take a charitable deduction of the fair-market value of the property contributed. The deduction is limited to 30% of the donor's adjusted gross income. If the fair-market value is greater than the donor can use in one year, the excess can be carried forward as a charitable deduction to be used over the next five years. In addition, the donor avoids capital gains tax on the profit that would have been taxable if the property had been sold, and the asset will not be subject to estate tax at the time of the donor's death.

- *Tangible property.* Coins, antique cars, jewelry, and other collectibles, all known as tangible personal property, may be accepted as gifts. The property must be saleable, and the donor must agree that the property can be sold unless the organization agrees to use the property in ways related to the organization's exempt purposes. The donor is responsible for obtaining a qualified appraisal in order to comply with IRS regulations. This gift to a charitable organization avoids capital gains tax, is deductible on the donor's income tax return, and removes the property from the donor's estate for estate tax purposes at the time of the donor's death.

- *Bargain sale.* A bargain sale is a sale of property by a donor to a charitable organization for a price less than the property's fair-market value. The excess of the fair-market value over the sales price represents a contribution, which is deductible by the donor for income tax purposes. The organization's board of directors should approve the purchase of property on a bargain sale basis. The amount of the allowable deduction for a bargain sale is subject to the rules of the IRS relating to bargain sales.

- *Charitable lead trusts.* A charitable lead trust is a separate legal entity that holds assets for a period of years or for the lives of one or more individuals for the benefit of a nonprofit organization, after which the assets are distributed by the trustee to noncharitable beneficiaries, often children or grandchildren, designated by the donor. During the period of the trust, it pays the trust income to the organization or to the organization's endowment—a wonderful way to build the endowment annually.

  The charitable lead trust is attractive to generous individuals in high estate and gift tax brackets. It allows the donor to benefit a favorite charity and, thereafter, pass the principal to family members with little or no taxes owed. A trust created during a donor's lifetime "locks in" the gift tax value early on, so any appreciation in value over the remaining years of the donor's life generally will not be taxed to the donor's estate or to the family.

Deferred Gifts

Some donors are reluctant to surrender control over assets that have been acquired over a lifetime. Others do not want to donate assets that generate earnings during their retirement years. Such donors can designate charitable organizations as the beneficiary of all or a portion of their assets at the time of their deaths. Such beneficiary designations are revocable. The donors may change the beneficiary at any time during their lifetimes. The overwhelming majority of donors, however, do not change beneficiaries once they are made.

- *Bequests by will or trust.* Bequests are the most common form of deferred gifts, accounting for approximately 80% of all deferred gifts each year. The donor should specify in a will or trust the organization as the donee and the name of the endowment fund to which the donor's gift should be allocated. Any restrictions on the use of the bequest may be described in detail in a separate fund agreement signed by both the donor and the organization.

Bequests can take many forms. Among the options available to donors are the following:

○ *Specific bequest.* The donor may give a specific sum of money, asset or list of assets, or real estate to the organization's endowment fund. Specific asset bequests offer certainty as to the asset or amount that will ultimately be given.

○ *Percentage bequest.* The donor directs a percentage of his or her estate to be given to the organization's endowment fund. This percentage could be of the donor's entire estate, residuary estate, or specific asset. By using a percentage, charitable gifts will automatically adjust with fluctuations in the size of the estate.

○ *Residuary bequest.* A provision in the will or trust that directs the remainder of the estate or a designated percentage of the remainder of the estate, after all other provisions in the will or trust are satisfied and all estate administrative costs are paid, to the organization's endowment fund is a residuary bequest to the organization. A residuary gift is a gift of "what's left" after all other gifts are completed and made.

○ *Contingent bequest.* Donors may provide in their wills or trusts that their assets be given to nonprofit organizations if those named as primary beneficiaries predecease the donor.

Charitable bequests require the assistance of a competent and independent attorney who is knowledgeable about state and federal laws governing wills, trusts, and charitable gifts. Preparation of a will or trust by someone other than a licensed attorney constitutes the unauthorized practice of law in all of the states. Thus, the nonprofit organization may want to keep a list of local attorneys who are experienced in charitable estate planning for donors who request referrals. As a caution, always recommend more than one attorney so that the organization does not appear to be soliciting clients for any particular attorney.

Although donors have no obligation to inform organizations about intended bequests, it is strongly recommended that donors consult with organizations' qualified staff to draft a description to guide the use of the gift. All communications with donors are held in strict confidence.

The organization will want to have sample bequest language, approved by its legal counsel, available to donors and their attorneys to ensure that bequests are properly designated.

Charitable bequests are deductible on the donor's estate tax return, thus passing free of estate taxes.

- *Life insurance.* Nonprofit organizations may accept gifts of life insurance policies. Donors may make gifts of paid-up life insurance policies to the organization and take a tax deduction for the interpolated terminal reserve (typically cash surrender value). Donors need an independent appraisal to claim the deduction. Or, donors may make gifts of premium-due policies to the organization and then take tax deductions for gifts to the organization to pay the premiums. In either case, the organization becomes the owner of the policy, names itself the beneficiary of the policy, and retains the policy in its offices. Before accepting a policy requiring ongoing premium payments, the organization and the donor should agree, in writing, on arrangements for the future payment of such premiums.

  The donor of the policy is entitled to an income tax deduction of the cash surrender value of the policy and another tax deduction for the annual premiums paid, if any, following the gift of the policy. The full face value of the policy can be added to the organization's endowment fund or used to establish a named fund as the donor requests.

  Alternatively, the donor may choose to retain ownership of the policy and name the organization as the beneficiary of the policy at the donor's death. In a written letter of agreement, the donor may direct the organization to add the policy proceeds to its endowment

TIPS & TECHNIQUES

Sample Language for Gifts by Bequest

(1) I give to (the exact legal name of the organization) ___ percent of the residue of my estate, real or personal, after payment of all bequests. Or (2) I give to (the exact legal name of the organization) the sum of $_____. Or (3) I give the residue of my estate, real or personal, to (the exact legal name of the organization). (The exact legal name of the organization) shall administer these assets as an endowed fund according to its Investment and Spending Policies. The annual distributions from such fund shall be used for the purpose of _____ (explain the purpose of the fund). The fund so established shall be known as the _____(name) Fund of (the exact legal name of the organization).

The language above is intended as an example only and should not be regarded as legal advice. Please check with the organization's attorney for exact legal language appropriate for each state.

fund and may even describe any restrictions on the use of the fund's earnings. Or, as with any gift, the donor may direct that the organization use the policy proceeds to create a new named fund. In both cases, the donor's estate will report the value of the policy on the federal estate tax return and thus take a charitable deduction for the value of the gift. Or, the donor can name the organization as a contingent beneficiary of a life insurance policy. The organization would receive the proceeds only if the donor's primary beneficiary died before the donor.

- *Retirement assets.* Retirement plans—including Individual Retirement Accounts (IRA), 401(k), 403(b), and other defined contribution plans—make tax-effective gifts to nonprofit organizations. Retirement funds are particularly attractive as charitable gifts because income taxes and, possibly, estate taxes will be due upon the death of the retirement asset owner. Depending on the size of the donor's taxable estate, more than 70% of retirement fund assets can end up passing to state and federal taxing authorities. Gifts of retirement assets can be made in several ways:

○ By naming the organization as a beneficiary for all or part of the assets upon the death of the retirement asset owner.

○ By naming the organization as the contingent beneficiary, thus giving heirs the right to "disclaim" (decline) retirement benefits in the organization's favor. Heirs who understand the impact of taxes on these assets may find it preferable to have the retirement assets pass 100% to a worthwhile cause.

○ By creating a testamentary charitable remainder trust with the assets, naming the organization as remainder beneficiary and non-charitable heirs as income beneficiaries.

Deferred Gifts with Income Benefits

Donors may make irrevocable gifts during their lifetimes in which they (or their chosen noncharitable beneficiaries) retain benefits during their lifetimes (or for a period of years) and the organizations receive the remaining assets. These gifts are sometimes called "split interest" gifts, because the donors and the organizations each have financial interests in the assets.

● *Charitable gift annuity.* A charitable gift annuity is a contract under which a charitable organization, in exchange for cash or other property, agrees to pay a fixed sum of money for a period measured by one or two lives. The person who contributes the asset for the annuity is called the "donor," and the person who receives the fixed payments is called the "annuitant." Usually, the donor and the annuitant are the same person, but this is not always true. A donor can make the contribution and direct the payments to her- or himself. Alternatively, the donor could direct that the payments be made to someone else (e.g., a sibling or parent). The maximum number of annuitants is two, and payments can be made to them jointly or successively.

Gift annuity payments can begin immediately after the contribution or begin on a future date, which is called a deferred-payment gift annuity. The longer the annuitant waits to start payments, the larger they will be. Whether a gift annuity is immediate or deferred, payments are fixed from the outset. They will neither increase nor decrease, no matter what happens to interest rates or the stock market. The organization is contractually obligated to make the payments, even if it has to dip into its general funds to do so. Fixed payments are a source of comfort to people who don't want their future security to be dependent on the performance of financial markets. The disadvantage of fixed payments is that they offer no inflation protection.

Small and midsized organizations may not want to offer gift annuities on their own, but rather partner with a larger institution such as a national affiliation or a community foundation.

Gift annuity rates are determined by the age of the person or persons who receive the income payments. The older the beneficiary, the higher the gift annuity rate. Although the exact rate may be negotiated, most nonprofits follow the rate provided by the American Council on Gift Annuities (*www.acga-web.org*).

Benefits to the donor include the following:

○ Income for life is at payout rates established for one or two lives.

○ A part of the gift is a current, deductible charitable gift.

○ A large portion of the annual payout is tax-free return of principal.

○ Capital gains tax savings are realized when appreciated assets are used for the gift.

○ Estate taxes are avoided on the gifted asset.

○ Personal satisfaction is obtained from making a gift of lasting significance.

- *Charitable remainder trust.* Charitable remainder trusts also offer income to the donor or other beneficiaries designated by the donor and are more complex to establish than a charitable gift annuity. There are two basic types, with numerous sophisticated variations possible.

  ○ *Charitable remainder unitrust.* With a charitable remainder unitrust, the donor irrevocably transfers money, securities, or other property to a trustee. Usually, the nonprofit organization does not serve as a trustee of a charitable remainder unitrust; that role belongs to a bank trust department or a brokerage firm selected by the donor— or the donor may be the trustee him- or herself. The trustee pays the donor (or one or more income beneficiaries designated by the donor) a fixed percentage of the net fair-market value of the trust's assets, as determined each year. The payments are made for the life or lives of the income beneficiaries or for a fixed period of years not to exceed 20 years. Upon termination of the income beneficiary's interest, the assets of the unitrust are transferred to the nonprofit organization.

  ○ *Charitable remainder annuity trust.* A charitable remainder annuity trust works like a unitrust except that the income beneficiary receives a fixed dollar amount annually from the trust. The amount distributed to the beneficiaries does not change as the value of the trust increases or decreases. The annuity trust is particularly attractive to people who want certainty about the amount of the annual payments.

    By establishing a charitable remainder trust, the donor can accomplish the following:

    • Establish an income for life—one that can grow, or shrink, over time (a unitrust) or one that will remain constant (an annuity trust).

    • Reinvest a highly appreciated low-yield asset, without incurring capital gain tax.

    • Reduce income taxes.

- Gain the investment and administrative services of a trustee.

- Get rid of the financial and personal burdens of managing the asset, especially in the case of real estate.

- Remove the asset from his or her estate.

- Make a magnificent gift to the organization's endowment fund.

Unlike charitable gift annuities, the assets of a charitable remainder trust may be exhausted and payments may cease.

- *Pooled income fund.* A pooled income fund accepts gifts from many donors, "pools" those funds together for investment purposes, and distributes the fund's earned income on a proportional basis to all participants or beneficiaries designated by the donors. When the named income beneficiary passes away, the portion of the fund's principal associated with the gift is added to the organization's endowment fund.

    Small and midsized organizations may not want to start their own pooled income fund, but rather partner with a larger institution such as a national affiliation or a community foundation. During times of generally low interest rates, many organizations do not offer pooled income funds.

    Donors to the pool receive charitable income tax deductions based on their ages at the time the gifts are made. The amount of the annual payout fluctuates with the value of the fund, so the donor may also gain a practical hedge against inflation. The gift may also produce estate tax savings, especially if the income beneficiaries are the donor and the donor's spouse.

- *Future interest (or retained life interest) in real estate.* A donor may make a gift of a personal residence or farm to the organization and retain the right to occupy the property until death. Upon the donor's death, the organization will own the entire interest in the property. The donor will receive an income tax deduction for the present value of the gift. The donor should obtain an independent appraisal of the value of the property and should commit, in writing, to pay the taxes, insurance, and upkeep on the property until the transfer of the property to the organization. These gifts should be evaluated by the organization's board of trustees and its counsel on a case-by-case basis.

The Donors' Desires Are Paramount

Whatever gift vehicles donors choose, those who make significant gifts to endowment do so for one or more of the reasons listed earlier in this chapter and in Chapter 4. Donors make gifts in their time frame, not necessarily the organization's. The gift reflects the donor's interests and values, not necessarily the needs of the organization. Be careful, however, that the organization does not stray from its mission in attempting to meet the donors' objectives. For example, a donor who wants to endow a new program at the zoo for rescued birds of prey could be redirected to the local veterinarian school or wildlife rescue operation—unless the zoo is already planning to establish such a program.

Fundraising professionals who are most successful at attracting endowment gifts for their organizations generally are able to focus their donor cultivation and solicitation programs around understanding the donor's concerns and passions, building a firm relationship with the donor, and linking the donor's urgent considerations with the organization's salient advantages, purposes, and programs.

A (Very Brief) History of Endowment

Endowments have existed since the time of the Romans. Research conducted at the University of Illinois Foundation reports that Marcus Aurelius, who ruled from 161–180 A.D., endowed a chair of rhetoric and four chairs of philosophy in Athens. In eighth-century Turkey, wealthy princes endowed professorial chairs in colleges and endowed funds that supported residential students. In the ninth century, rajas endowed schools to promote learning, leading to the rise of Indian sciences, mathematics, and astronomy. At the same time in the Muslim world, rulers and princes provided the funds to build large public and private libraries.[8]

Eight hundred years later, a young minister named John Harvard died in 1638 and left his library and half his estate to a new institution designed to educate clergy in New England. He said that his gift was intended "to advance learning and perpetuate it to prosperity, dreading to leave an illiterate ministry."[9] When the College of William and Mary was being formed in 1693, James Blair, the College's founding president, was sent to England to seek both a charter and an endowment.[10]

Since the beginning of our nation, many charitable organizations have built endowments that provide annual support for their programs. The Metropolitan Museum of Art, for example, began its General Endowment Fund by motion of its board in May 1905, and it held assets of $302,115.29 by the end of that year. At the end of 2003, the Met held endowed funds of nearly $1.8 billion. Shriners Hospitals for Children started its endowment shortly after it was established in the early 1920s; its endowment was valued at $7.3 billion by 2004. By the beginning of 2004, The Nature Conservancy, established in 1951, held endowed assets of $633 million.

Because nonprofit organizations in the United States are not required by law to report the value of their endowments, it is impossible to accurately report the size of endowment assets. The 2003 National Association of College and University Business Officers' (NACUBO) Endowment Study[11] documented $230.5 billion in total endowment assets at 723 responding colleges and universities. According to a survey by *The Chronicle of Higher Education* and *The Chronicle of Philanthropy* in their 2004 publication "Endowments,"[12] the endowments of 187 of the nation's largest foundations, universities, hospitals, and other nonprofit organizations increased by $23.1 billion in 2003 alone. Harvard University held more than $23 billion in endowments at the end of fiscal year 2004—the largest of any university.

Yet, as we have seen, many established and important charitable organizations have inadequate endowment resources to provide for their preferred future. This book provides ideas and tools to nonprofit organizations that want to provide long-term support for their missions and goals.

Where Do We Go from Here?

This first chapter discussed the value of endowments to nonprofit organizations, donors, and fundraisers; offered concise definitions of the three types of endowments; and described the kinds of gifts and gift vehicles available to endowment donors and the benefits of each. It concluded with a brief review of the longevity and scope of endowments from ancient times to the present. In the next chapter, factors to successfully build an endowment, techniques to assess readiness for building endowments, ways to enlist champion volunteers, and considerations in establishing an endowment committee are presented.

Notes

1. *The Chronicle of Philanthropy*, Washington, D.C. *http://philanthropy.com*

2. Lynda S. Moerschbaecher. *Building an Endowment Right from the Start.* Chicago, IL: Precept Press, 2001.

3. Janne G. Gallagher. "Legal Briefs." *Foundation News and Commentary.* Volume 44, No. 2, March/April, 2003. Washington, D.C.: Council on Foundations.

4. National Conference of Commissioners on Uniform State Laws, "Uniform Management of Institutional Funds Act," 1972.

5. Association of Fundraising Professionals, AFP Survey Course Faculty Manual, Module G: Planned Giving, Revised 2002.

6. Paul G. Schervish, Preface, *The Complete Guide to Planned Giving* by Debra Ashton. Quincy, MA: Ashton Associates, 2004, p. ix.

7. Frank Minton, as quoted by William J. Moran in "Jump Start Your Planned Giving Program: Launch an Endowment Campaign," National Conference on Planned Giving, 1996.

8. Kay Bock, "Endowment—Foundation of Enlightenment," University of Illinois Foundation, 1997.

9. *www.aad.harvard.edu/pgo/html/index/htm*

10. *http://wm.edu/about/index*

11. *www.nacubo.org*

12. "Endowments." *The Chronicle of Higher Education* and *The Chronicle of Philanthropy.* Washington, D.C.,

CHAPTER 2

Preplanning and Assessing Readiness for Endowment

After reading this chapter, you will be able to

- List the key success factors in building endowment assets.
- Measure the organization's readiness for endowment building.
- Decide whether and how to conduct a fundraising assessment.
- Attract and retain endowment champions.
- Consider the advantages and drawbacks of establishing an endowment committee.
- Overcome concerns about building endowments.
- Build capacity to start the endowment building process.

A hundred times every day I remind myself that my inner and outer life are based on the labors of other men, living and dead, and that I must exert myself in order to give in the same measure as I have received and am still receiving.

—Albert Einstein

Building an endowment is a specialized form of fundraising that is critically important for many organizations and inappropriate for others. This chapter discusses the signs of organizational readiness to launch an endowment, factors in deciding whether to conduct a fundraising assessment, the importance of attracting and retaining endowment champions, the justification for and responsibilities of endowment committees, and ways that organizations increase capacity and determination to start the endowment building process.

Prime Factors in Successful Endowment Building

There are no cut-and-dried standards to determine whether an organization is ready and able to build an endowment, but there are several elements to measure. Each nonprofit organization that contemplates an endowment building program will want to evaluate the strength of its organization in the following areas, listed in order of importance:

- *The board of directors and staff are committed to building the endowment.* The board of directors should resolve that an endowment is a priority for the organization. The board and key staff members must understand that endowment building is a long-term process. Board and staff members need patience to match their understanding. Board members should commit themselves to meeting the future financial needs of the organization through building endowment. Board member support should include individual gifts, volunteer time, budget management, and the demand for reasonable results.

- *Leaders (staff and volunteer) are stable, knowledgeable, adequate, and available.* Committed leaders are willing to devote their time and skills to the various tasks required to implement endowment building strategies. Potential endowment champions and creative leaders are involved with the organization's fundraising program. Competent, qualified staff is available to plan endowment programs and to provide support to volunteers. Training and continuing education is provided and expected. Endowment building is included in job descriptions, and work is measured by more than the amount of money that is actually received each year. (See Chapter 8.)

- *The organization is strong, has a clear mission, and is considered worthy of philanthropic support.* The organization has earned the respect of its constituents. There is a history of strong program growth over the period of the organization's existence, generally at least eight to ten years. The organization has a written strategic plan that includes mission, goals, objectives, specific programs, and budgets for the organization for the next three, four, or five years. The organization has the capacity to commit current resources (both financial and personnel) for ongoing support of the organization's future.

- *The organization has a compelling case for future support.* The case for building an endowment must spell out specific programmatic, fundraising, and investment goals in a way that appeals to potential donors. The organization expects that its mission and work will continue in perpetuity. The well-articulated case describes gifts to the endowment as philanthropic investments that strengthen the organization's capacity to do something important. It describes how the endowment's earnings will impact people. It is an inspirational call to action, focused on the prospective donors' charitable objectives and desire to help people, not the organization's needs. As James Lord says in *The Raising of Money,* "Organizations don't have needs. People have needs."[1] Board, staff, and other key leaders are able to express the case in exciting terms that communicate their own commitments.

- *A solid fundraising program is in place.* The organization receives broad-based support from a growing annual fund program with solid repeat donors, major gifts, and a readiness to enter into planned giving. Prospective donors are offered multiple ways to support the organization through print and electronic direct mail, special events, and face-to-face visits by a development officer, board member, or the CEO. The process for researching, cultivating, soliciting, and thanking donors is accurate, effective, and timely. The day-to-day administration and management of the fundraising efforts are sound. Prospect and donor record-keeping systems provide storage and retrieval of essential data on donors in an expedient manner. (See Chapter 3.)

- *Substantial gifts inspire generous contributions from others.* The organization has experience in attracting major gift support for current programs and for capital purposes—and it has an ongoing process to identify, cultivate, and solicit prospective major donors. Its fundraising programs have attracted substantial gifts from individuals, foundations, corporations, associations, and governmental entities. The organization has compiled a list of potential major donors, primarily individuals and families. The organization has donors and prospects who are over age 50 and have accumulated assets during their lifetimes. It has already received gifts or commitments for gifts from individuals who have made an "ultimate" or sacrificial gift.

- *A constituency-wide marketing and communications plan is in place.* The organization's marketing plan, soundly conceived and implemented to involve people in a supportive relationship with the organization, is designed to develop acceptance of and excitement about the organization within the community. Present donors are considered a special constituency, and their involvement is carefully developed through two-way communications. The marketing and communications plan is able to expand to include messages and markets relevant to the endowment. (See Chapter 7.)

- *Written endowment policies are established.* Endowment policies are approved by the board. The endowment policy notebook should include investment and spending policies, selection of investment managers, standards for monitoring results, gift acceptance policies, and requirements for fund documentation. Procedures are documented in the notebook for such tasks as the administration of gifts and the authority to negotiate gifts and fund agreements. Guidelines are in place regarding named endowment funds, allowable restrictions on the use of funds, recognition and stewardship protocol, and donor designations. (See Chapter 5.)

Few, if any, organizations will rate high in every one of these areas, but each area should be carefully weighed and measured. Those listed first are often the most critical. Organizations that have multiple gaps in the areas listed may want to focus efforts to strengthen weaknesses before launching an endowment. See Tips & Techniques to measure how your organization rates in endowment readiness.

 TIPS & TECHNIQUES

Endowment Readiness Test

Consider the following test for endowment readiness, adapted with permission from Jacquelyn B. Ostrom's presentation at the Association of Fundraising Professionals' 2004 International Conference in Seattle.[2]

Range of Score	Your Organization's Score	
0–20	_____	Board commitment to endowment
0–20	_____	Knowledgeable leaders
0–15	_____	Strong organization
0–15	_____	Meritorious case for future support
0–10	_____	Solid fundraising program
0–10	_____	Substantial gifts
0–5	_____	Marketing program
0–5	_____	Endowment policies

100 is the maximum score. The criteria listed first are considered the most important. Usually, a score of at least 70 is necessary to successfully launch an endowment. If an organization is not ready to launch an endowment building program, it should undertake the work necessary to strengthen each area of weakness.

Organizations That Should Not Establish Endowments

While there are no firm rules, the following types of organizations generally should not attempt to launch an endowment:

- Startups

- Temporary organizations

- Those that are not financially viable or whose annual fundraising results fall short of budget

- Those whose board and staff members do not understand that endowment building takes time and patience

- Those that are unable or unwilling to spend current resources for future support

- Those without knowledgeable and adequate development staff and board members

- Those who are looking for the pot of gold at the end of the rainbow that will fix all of the organization's shortcomings and problems

Requirements of Development Officers

Development officers, even those with years of experience working with major gift donors, are often hesitant to initiate an endowment building effort. Their questions include the following:

- What do I need to know?

- How do I get ready?

- How much of my time will I need to devote to it?

- How will my boss evaluate this work?

- How will I keep score until the money arrives?

These (and more) questions are important to address. Some are discussed in other chapters. For example, Chapter 8 describes performance indicators that should be used to assess the work of the development officers, especially in the early years before many gifts have been received.

The most important qualifications for endowment officers are (1) passionate belief in the organization's mission and work and (2) genuine interest in people and the ability to elicit their values and charitable interests. An understanding of financial matters, a master's degree in marketing, five years of experience as a tax attorney, a background in planned giving, or graduate training in psychology would be valuable, but is not necessary

An interest in learning about endowments, major gift fundraising, and planned giving is essential. Nearly everyone has access to the resources needed to become conversant with important concepts and terminology. Many training opportunities will focus on planned giving or major gift donors, rather than endowment building. Nonetheless, development officers will acquire the skills and tools they need.

Begin by locating the nearest local planned giving counsel at *www.ncpg.org*. Attend its meetings, both for the content of the presentations and to meet others who work in the planned giving arena. Develop a support network of experienced planned giving colleagues and professional advisors experienced in gift planning techniques on whom to call with questions or for advice.

If not already a member, join the local chapter of the Association of Fundraising Professionals (*www.afpnet.org*). They, too, sponsor a wide range of monthly meetings, seminars, conferences, and online materials.

The Internet offers a plethora of resources. Many articles and several books have been written about endowments. Check with the professional associations with which the nonprofit organization is affiliated. Numerous planned giving vendors offer preprinted materials to send to prospective donors and advisors. *Planned Giving Mentor* is a monthly newsletter for newcomers to gift planning and offers examples of its articles at *www.pgmentor.com*. (In the interest of full disclosure, the author is a member of the National Board of Gift Planning Consultants for *Planned Giving Mentor.*)

The amount of time that staff must devote to endowment building depends on the organization's goals for each program. In their monthly newsletters, some organizations simply encourage donors to make a charitable bequest and wait for the donors to respond. This is a start and takes very little time. Other organizations assign an existing development staff member to devote 10% to 50% of his or her work to endowment building. As a general rule, at least one day a week needs to be focused on endowment building efforts in order to realize sustained and measurable growth. Many organizations have found that hiring full-time professional development staff to build endowment is an effective investment of resources over time when measured against gifts received, expectancies confirmed, and the value of the endowment

Fundraising Assessment

Many organizations that have decided to begin or renew an endowment building effort start with a fundraising assessment of their overall fundraising program. The endowment efforts should be integrated into all philanthropic opportunities offered to prospective donors. Otherwise, the endowment effort can become isolated, even insulated, from the overall development plans and the work of staff members and volunteers.

Purpose of the Assessment

While a comprehensive fundraising assessment serves as a guide for the organization in all its fundraising priorities and strategies, this book is focused on the assessment's value to endowment building. A quality assessment enables board and staff members:

- To decide where the endowment program fits into the organization's comprehensive development program.

- To determine the relative importance of the endowment program to the organization.

- To determine the relative importance of the endowment program to current and prospective donors.

- To identify issues that need to be addressed before establishing or reinvigorating an endowment.

- To make people feel connected to the proposed endowment program.

- To identify what people want from your organization and what they expect its endowment to accomplish.

- To determine how the organization is viewed by participants in the assessment. As a leader in its field? An important player in the community? Warm and welcoming to constituents?

- To determine if your case for the endowment is in sync with your donors' interests.

Assessors

The assessment can be conducted by staff members or by outside consultants. If it is done internally by one or more staff members, they have the advantage of already knowing the institution and its constituents. Moreover, the expenses for the study will be minimal. The risk of using staff members to conduct a study is that interviewees may be less than candid about the organization for fear of offending the staff. An outside consultant can generally bring objectivity to the study and gain more information from the interviews. Consultants also bring experience with other organizations and similar fundraising programs—and may have additional credibility with board and community members. However, the consultant will need to learn about the organization and its values, programs, and constituents, and the consultant will charge a fee for services.

When choosing a consultant, check with peer organizations for recommendations. Conduct a preliminary interview to explain the project and gain an initial impression about the consultant who will actually be doing the work. Ask the consultant to submit a written proposal and a list of references. Follow up and contact every reference with questions about the consultant's performance and effectiveness.

Assessment Methodology

A fundraising assessment will use several methods to gather relevant data:

- *Personal and telephone interviews.* A one-on-one interview, preferably in person, with selected individuals including board members, staff members, major donors, and community leaders is the most effective method to gather reliable opinions about the organization. Scheduled to last 30 to 60 minutes, the interview can explore the relationship between the individual and the organization and his or her perceptions of the organization's strengths and weaknesses, opinions of its fundraising efforts, experiences as a donor, commitment to the organization's mission and goals, likelihood of future gifts, willingness to serve in a volunteer capacity, and other selected topics. Persons interviewed may be asked to comment about the organization, the proposed goals for the endowment, and the organization's proposed plan of action. They may also be asked to identify prospects, to nominate leaders, and to give an indication of the size of gift they might make.

- *Group meetings.* A gathering of a small group of constituents (approximately 8 to 12 people) with an established set of questions is a widely used method to elicit personal opinions and discover levels of commitment. These focused discussions can pull information from participants that might not surface in an individual interview. Attitudes, beliefs, opinions, motivations, and reactions can be explored. Participants have the opportunity to disclose their perceptions of the organization and their reaction to its case for the endowment. People often piggyback their own ideas onto the comments made by others in the group. These gatherings can be structured with experienced facilitators or can simply be lunches in a quiet location with small groups made up of a few (carefully selected) people. Organizations with regional or national constituencies have tried to accomplish the same results with conference calls, but they generally work poorly and are not recommended.

- *The collection and review of print and electronic materials.* Strategic plans, annual reports, financial statements, gift histories, annual budgets, fundraising letters and invitations, stewardship materials and reports, and other documents related to fundraising provide the assessor with background information about the organization's fundraising practices. These materials provide valuable historic context for the assessor, as well as the basis for the recommendations to follow.

- *Research to identify funding patterns and fundraising strategies of comparable organizations.* The assessor can gather publicly available data from national and regional associations identified by the organization's leaders and from IRS Form 990 informational tax returns filed by comparable organizations. The assessor can then select those that seem the most similar for in-depth analyses, often including a telephone interview with the CEO or development director. These data are used to establish realistic expectations for the organization as well as examples of strategies that have worked for peer organizations.

Assessment Report

An assessment concludes with a written report of findings and recommendations designed to assist the organization to make decisions on the scope and size of the endowment building program. It will identify gift potential, provide guidance to establish realistic goals and objectives, and suggest a time frame to reach the overall goal. It will test the case for endowment support and determine what kinds of endowment funds the institution should encourage.

The assessment will help leadership determine the system for prospect identification and cultivation, the specific gift techniques that may be pursued (e.g., current gifts, bequests, gift annuities), and identify special gift opportunities and problem areas that may inhibit donors. It will identify volunteer leadership—with the potential to give and the ability to solicit other substantial donors—and a core list of prospective donors. Recommended promotional activities will be discussed. Indicators of internal readiness—staff, data management, donor files, and policies—will be evaluated and budget requirements will be analyzed.

The fundraising assessment presells the organization's future needs and its endowment program to major prospects who were selected for the initial round of interviews. This preselling (everyone likes to be involved in creating and planning future programs) will likely accelerate the involvement and cultivation of those involved in the assessment.

After the assessment is complete, the board should commit a meeting, or meetings, to receive and analyze the report. Thereafter, if the board decides to proceed with an endowment building program, the organization should develop a multiyear strategy to build the endowment. The creation of the strategy is discussed in Chapter 3.

Endowment Champions

The endowment building program needs more than competent leadership; it needs excited and engaged *champions* on the board and as volunteers. Champions are financial contributors who are models for others to emulate *and* who are willing to talk about their own commitment.

These champions are the most important components of the organization's leadership team. They set the pace for others. They lead by example. They meet with friends, neighbors, colleagues, and others to describe the importance of the endowment, the difference it will make in the community, and their

IN THE REAL WORLD

Deciding to Build
an Endowment

When I asked the board of trustees of a large San Francisco Bay Area church if they wished to encourage endowment gifts, the verbal equivalent of a food fight broke out. They let fly with arguments pro and con, more-or-less along the following lines:

"We don't want our hands tied by donors' restricting their bequests to endowments."

"But we'll never grow up as an organization if we keep plowing bequests into operating expenses."

"Yeah, but what if we're in the red at the end of the year, and it's either use a bequest or let go of staff?"

"The reason we keep facing red ink is that our endowment is so pathetic."

"So you want donors telling us how to use their bequests?"

"That's their right, and making a bequest that won't get burnt in six months is something more and more donors want to do."

"But our congregation members don't think that way."

"Well, I'm a member of the congregation, and I do!"

"Endowments are to congregations what life support is to a patient in a hopeless coma. If the congregation isn't willing to support itself, let it die of natural causes."

"The people who built this church seventy years ago sure didn't think that way. This church building is *our* inheritance. What are *we* leaving to the future?"

So the argument went, rumbling along inconclusively until it bumped into the next agenda item. The board president, a tight smile creasing his

IN THE REAL WORLD (CONTINUED)

face, asked me and the planned giving committee to come back to the board with an endowment policy draft.

Some months later, the board had developed a clearly defined capital and endowment campaign. The process hadn't been pretty, but they had moved from food fight to love feast.

[Phil Murphy, a planned giving specialist in San Anselmo, California.]

own decision-making process to make a significant financial contribution to it. They have credibility and clout with their peers.

Identification of Champions

After the decision to build an endowment has been made and the prospects have been identified, the most important function for senior staff and board members is to identify the potential champions—those to whom the prospects cannot say "no." The first place to look is at the board. Consider the members who were the most enthusiastic and articulate about the importance of building an endowment. Often, one or two people led the effort to convince the board to start or renew the endowment. Talk with those people about the importance of their continued enthusiasm, leadership, and commitment to recruiting a core group of champions to lead the endowment building effort. The endowment chair or cochairs are often most effective if they are also board members. Cochairs for the endowment program can often share responsibility, balance each other's strengths and weaknesses, and offer complementary skills and insights.

Other endowment champions can be found in the ranks of former board members, volunteers, and long-term supporters. Often the fundraising assessment uncovers individuals who care deeply about the institution and its long-term viability. The endowment chair or cochairs will want to meet individually with selected people to engage them in the challenge and excitement of building the endowment.

Before the organization has recruited and trained its endowment champions, the staff members need to serve as endowment leaders to articulate the organization's values, the case for endowment support, and the benefits that an endowment will offer. Although staff members may be impassioned leaders and advocates for the endowment, they cannot substitute for volunteer champions and should step back from the leadership role as soon as champions are in place.

Involvement of Champions

Offer endowment champions a variety of ways to be involved, encouraging them to decide how they can be most effective.

- *Endowment committee.* An endowment committee is the traditional way to organize all programs and activities related to endowment building, which is discussed in the next section. It is important to note, however, that some endowment champions may chose not to serve on any committee or may not have time for regularly scheduled commitments.

- *Personal visits.* Face-to-face visits with people known to the champion are the most effective methods to generate gifts for endowment. Some endowment chairs promise their champions that they will not have to attend any committee meetings if they agree to be on-call for visits.

- *Group presentations.* Some champions serve as speakers for appropriate social and civic groups in the community about the organization, its current programs, the endowment effort, and a personal testimonial about why they are committed to growing the endowment.

- *Host gatherings.* Other champions will be more comfortable hosting a group of people in their own homes or in a neutral location such as a community center, church, or library.

- *Solicit gifts.* Yes, the champions must ask for gifts. (See Chapter 4.)

Endowment Committees

Before establishing an endowment committee, carefully consider its function and whether another committee is already charged to do the job at hand or whether new tasks could be assigned to an existing committee—perhaps the development committee, the long-range planning committee, or the executive committee. Larger organizations may already have a planned giving committee that could undertake endowment building responsibilities. When the development staff is already overburdened with responsibilities to the board and possibly a development committee, a new committee is sometimes the last thing that the staff or the organization needs.

In other situations, an endowment committee is needed to provide leadership, credibility, and guidance for the endowment program and to offer support and training for endowment champions and volunteers. An endowment committee should be carefully organized and careful to use its members' time and expertise effectively.

Functions

The board chair (or the endowment committee chair) should establish the functions of the committee at the outset. The functions might include the following:

- Provide guidance for the endowment building program and its promotion.

- Test the case for support.

- Act as a lead-gathering and lead-analysis source by bringing suggestions of prospective contributors to the meetings and rating or screening prospects.

- Provide introductions to potential donors and professional advisors for the staff.

- Attend personal visits with prospective donors, alone, or with other committee members, or with staff.

- Solicit gifts.

- Using professional expertise and experience, write articles for the organization's newsletter or other publications about estate planning, charitable giving, planned giving vehicles, and endowment building techniques.

- Provide hands-on volunteer assistance with special events, publications, mailings, scheduling, and so forth.

Committee Composition

In addition to the chair or cochairs, the committee should include people who have high visibility and extensive acquaintance with many of the prospective donors and legal and financial professionals. All should be current contributors and prospective endowment donors.

Responsibilities of Committee Members

Committee members provide validity, continuity, and credibility to the endowment program. They need to understand what is expected of them. Committee members deserve a written job description with time commitment, responsibilities, and expectations clearly spelled out. A job description also helps avoid confusion or disappointment later. Some of the responsibilities of committee members include the following:

- Make own gift to the endowment.

- Review and approve recommended strategies to grow the endowment.

- Represent the organization and the endowment program to the broader community.

- Identify and cultivate potential contributors.

- Team with the staff to visit prospective donors.
- Work with the staff to promote the endowment in the community.

Meetings

The endowment committee should have regularly scheduled meetings with a written agenda and related materials sent or e-mailed in advance. Members need to know that each meeting is important and that it is important that each person is there. Do not hold a meeting if there is no business to conduct or no compelling reason to meet face to face. Cancel the meeting—with at least three days' notice if possible—and the development officer will have a grateful committee.

Give people a reason to be at each meeting in person. Provide a tour, a guest speaker, or an engaging discussion. Don't ask people to come if they could have read a report at home instead. You want the committee members to leave the meeting saying, "If I had not shown up, I'd have missed that."

Don't Let Myths Get in the Way

Board or staff members will probably bring up one or more of the following "urban legends" and legitimate concerns. Leadership's job is to determine which statements are worth worrying about and how the organization can mitigate their effects.

"Endowments Are a Sign of Too Many Riches."

Some people claim that endowments are simply a form of saving for future expenditure rather than using donations for current purposes—and that organizations' current contributions should be used for programs now. If organizations choose to set aside some of their revenue as endowments or spend resources attracting endowment gifts, they must have more money than they need to achieve their missions.

However, with the decrease of federal and state expenditures for most cultural, social services, educational, and health care nonprofits in the past decade, organizations are increasingly faced with greater demand for services without commensurate increases in revenue. In his article in the May 27, 2004 issue of *The Chronicle of Philanthropy*, Dennis R. Hammond states:

> Prudence demands, and common law encourages, institutions to set aside some of each year's unspent earnings, together with gifts given in perpetuity, to help maintain operations in future years when revenues, earnings, and gifts to the annual fund are inadequate. . . . There will be inevitable periods of conflict between short-term operational needs and the long-term need for growth and maintenance. Board members must evaluate their institutions' idiosyncratic needs during market or operational shocks. But in that ambiguous art of balancing present and future demands, one fact remains unambiguous: Endowments are not a luxury but a necessity.[3]

"Donors Who Contribute to the Endowment Will Decrease the Amount of or Discontinue Their Annual Gift."

This old fear has proven to be groundless. Endowment donors, with few exceptions, are long-term contributors to annual fund campaigns who decide to also provide lasting endowment gifts. Once their endowment gifts are completed or pledged, they usually are even more committed to the organization and its ongoing operating needs. Time and again, capital and endowment campaigns raise the level of annual giving, not reduce it.

"Endowment Building Relies on Direct Cultivation and Solicitation of Prospective Donors by Staff Members."

Endowment building requires in-depth knowledge about the organization, the cultivation of long-term relationships, broad understanding of planned giving options, exceptional stewardship of the donor and the gift, and personal contact with prospective and current donors.

Often it involves partnerships between volunteer endowment champions and staff members, especially in the initial stages of cultivation. The volunteer may know the prospective donor personally and have greater knowledge about the organization's programs than a relatively new staff member, while the staff member understands the nuances of various gift planning techniques and the institution's investment policies. Once the prospective donor is comfortable with and confident in the staff member, the volunteer's role lessens—thus freeing the volunteer to introduce another prospective donor to the organization.

Endowment building relies on consistent face-to-face visits with current and prospective donors over time. This disciplined effort usually falls to the staff. Some donors do not feel comfortable discussing their personal finances with a friend; they may be more likely to do so with a trained staff member.

"It Takes Too Long to See Results."

Endowment building can be a slow process. Frequently, endowment gifts can take 12 to 24 months from cultivation through gift completion—and, if they are deferred gifts, actual receipt of the assets may take many additional years. However, the amount of the gift is often substantial (10 to 1,000 times the donor's average annual gift).

Endowment building is not for those who need to see quick results. Some volunteers and staff members always tackle other tasks with more immediate gratification and never find the time for long-term gift cultivation, negotiation, and completion. They, however, will not experience the pleasure of witnessing the joy in donors' eyes as they finalize endowment gifts that will provide benefits to people who are not yet born.

"The Organization Has to Spend Resources Now for Gifts That May Not Be Realized for Years."

Yes, the commitment of time and money to cultivate and solicit gifts, prepare and review paperwork, establish policies and procedures, screen potential gifts, administer the endowment, oversee its investment, and thank and steward donors must be considered at the beginning of the endowment building process. Endowment building requires an investment of resources on the part of the organization. It also holds the promise of building a pipeline of assets that will be received by the organization in the future to provide necessary support in lean years and the possibility of new programs and services in more prosperous times.

Where Do We Go from Here?

Before an organization decides to commit itself and its resources to building an endowment, the organization must carefully look at its readiness and willingness to undertake this work, with full knowledge of the challenge ahead, the issues it faces, and the long-term commitment required. Without a realistic assessment of its ability to raise endowment gifts, the organization's commitment to building an endowment is likely to be only a paper tiger.

The next chapter describes the process of developing an Endowment Action Program to guide the organization as it goes about the business of raising a significant endowment and offers several Tips & Techniques to ensure that the plan is put into practice and is able to be adapted to changing circumstances down the road.

Notes

1. James G. Lord. *The Raising of Money.* Cleveland, OH: Third Sector Press, 1983.

2. Jacquelyn B. Ostrom. "The Ultimate in Nonprofit Sustainability: Raising Endowment Dollars." 2004 AFP International Conference, March 17, 2004, Seattle, WA.

3. Dennis R. Hammond, "Endowments Are Not a Luxury," *The Chronicle of Philanthropy*, May 27–28, 2004, p. B26.

CHAPTER 3

Developing the Case for Support and the Endowment Action Program

After reading this chapter, you will be able to

- Design a comprehensive Endowment Action Program.
- Garner the enthusiastic support of the board.
- Define the case for endowment support.
- Develop measurable goals, strategies, and tactics to reach the goals.
- Establish a realistic time frame.
- Consider staff and budget requirements.

People want to be part of something that makes a difference, that transcends the ordinary. They want a star to steer by. They need a clear, compelling mission—a reason for being, a purpose.

—Frances Hesselbein

*Plans are only good intentions unless they immediately degenerate
into hard work.*

—Peter F. Drucker

Once the organization has determined that it is ready to move forward with building or reinvigorating its endowment, the real work begins to develop a comprehensive Endowment Action Program. This work starts with a board resolution designed to integrate the endowment into the organization's strategic plan. It includes the case for support, measurable goals, strategies and tactics to reach the goals, and the time frame, as well as staff and budget requirements. Other components of the Endowment Action Program—working with prospective donors (Chapter 4), management and investment of gifts (Chapter 5), donor and volunteer stewardship and recognition (Chapter 6), marketing (Chapter 7), and evaluation (Chapter 8)—are discussed at length in separate chapters.

The Importance of the Endowment Action Program

Resistance, in one form or another, often results when a new program is introduced or a dormant program is revived. The Endowment Action Program serves two functions: (1) it attacks the resistance and (2) it provides a blueprint to reach agreed-upon goals.

The development and adoption of an Endowment Action Program (the Action Program) involves the very people—board and staff members, donors, constituents, and community members—who will be essential to its successful implementation. The involvement of those people in the design of the Action Program is essential to organization-wide understanding and support for building the endowment. Board and staff members—within the development department and in other departments—are more likely to carry out strategies if they have a voice in designing the strategies. The process of developing the Action Program should include the identification of potential endowment champions and donors.

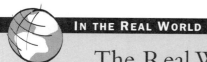

The Real World Wants Action

"We don't need a *plan* that will gather dust on a shelf," declared Thomas Courtice, then the president of Ohio Wesleyan University. "We want a *campaign*, with realistic goals, and strategies and tactics to reach the goals."

I was meeting with a small group of board members from the Community Foundation of Delaware County to discuss my proposal to assist the board with its assessment of the Foundation's current asset development and communications activities and to help in the design of a comprehensive five-year asset development plan for the Foundation. While I agreed with Dr. Courtice that written plans are never effective if they are not implemented, I was concerned that the term "campaign" implied a set time frame. I know that endowment building is a long-term process.

"Let's call it an 'Action Program,'" he suggested. "I want the board to understand that this is an ongoing program that requires the commitment of all of us to take specific actions if we expect our assets to grow."

Since that conversation, I no longer think in terms of strategic plans or endowment campaigns. Endowment Action Programs are now the norm.

Endorsement and Enthusiasm of the Board of Directors

The board of directors must embrace the value of an endowment to the organization. It must be willing to commit the resources and time necessary to generate the endowment. It must accept its role in growing the endowment.

Enlisting the Board's Support

Consider a variety of approaches to garner the board's support:

- Share the results of the assessment study.

- Gather information about successful endowment programs at other similar institutions.

- Ask a planned giving consultant, professional advisor, someone who has made a significant gift to another organization, or a prominent person to give a presentation to the board about endowments.

- Ask the board chair, CEO, or development director of a respected local organization to talk to the board about the value of their endowment to their institution.

- Involve board members in developing the case for endowment support, as described in a following section.

- Send current board members who "get it" to recruit new board members.

Board Resolution to Build an Endowment

One way to ensure that the board as a whole focuses on the importance of an endowment is to propose that it pass a resolution to build an endowment and integrate it into all facets of the organization's fundraising efforts. In the course of passing such a resolution, the board should discuss and reach an agreement on the purposes of the endowment and what it intends that the endowment will provide for the organization in the future. The board should reach an agreement about whether the endowment will operate as a true endowment, quasi-endowment, term endowment, or all three (see Chapter 1).

Responsibilities of the Board of Directors

The board of directors assumes additional responsibilities when it decides to build an endowment. First, it must adopt policies related to endowment gifts and the investment of the assets (see Chapter 5). Second, it must periodically review those policies and oversee investment performance against established

TIPS & TECHNIQUES

Sample Resolution to Build an Endowment

WHEREAS, Any Charity, Inc., an Ohio not-for-profit corporation, was established on September 16, 1964 for charitable, educational, and public purposes; and

WHEREAS, the mission and vision of Any Charity, Inc. are vitally important to the people served by Any Charity, Inc.;

NOW THEREFORE IT IS RESOLVED, that Any Charity, Inc. will establish for the benefit of Any Charity, Inc., a permanent endowment, named the Any Charity, Inc. Endowment, to provide an ongoing source of support, to enhance its stability and prestige, to fund its program expansion, to provide financial independence from outside forces, and to offer flexibility for its management; and

RESOLVED FURTHER, that Any Charity, Inc. shall allocate resources, both in time and money, to the growth of the endowment; and

RESOLVED FURTHER, that Any Charity, Inc., shall adopt the Endowment Action Program attached hereto and integrate it into all of its fundraising programs and activities, and shall actively educate clients, members, volunteers, donors, gift planners, and other constituents about the endowment and methods to contribute toward its growth.

benchmarks. Third, it must allocate adequate resources (i.e., board and staff time, money, office space) so that the endowment will achieve its purposes.

Responsibilities of Individual Board Members

Individual board members have additional responsibilities when the organization creates an endowment. These responsibilities fall on all members and are included in board member job descriptions. These responsibilities include the following:

- Meet with staff members and professional advisors to learn more about giving opportunities to the endowment.

- Make a personal financial commitment, either current or deferred, to the endowment.

- Approve the purposes and restrictions of proposed gifts.

- Introduce the organization, other board members, and the staff to colleagues and acquaintances who may be prospective endowment contributors.

Unrestricted Memorial and Planned Gifts

The board should adopt a policy to add unrestricted planned gifts and memorial gifts to its quasi-endowment fund. It is important that such a policy is adopted before a gift is on the table because future boards will be sorely tempted to direct matured planned gifts to a variety of current needs and opportunities rather than to the growth of the endowment. The policy will evoke careful attention by the board to each such gift. Of course, a future board could change the policy at any time. (See Appendix E, Sample Acceptance Policies for Endowment Gifts, for draft language.)

Named Endowment Agreements

The board should approve the form of a draft named endowment agreement before prospective donor cultivation and solicitation are initiated so that the organization's representative can share the draft language with prospective donors and their professional advisors. Usually, a committee of the board (perhaps the development or endowment committee) prepares the draft for the board's review and adoption. (See Tips & Techniques in Chapter 5 for a sample.)

The Case for Endowment Support

There are no million-dollar gifts without million-dollar dreams—both the donor's and the organization's. The case for support defines the organization's dreams and aspirations.

The organization's mission distinguishes it from another organization. The mission defines the organization and provides the distinctive edge that attracts support. Donors and their advisors want to be assured that the mission will be as valued 50 years from now as it is today. Endowment donors give to the future of the organization and must be comfortable with the long-term value and viability of the organization and its mission.

The organization may already have a compelling case for annual support or for support of a capital campaign, but the endowment fund needs its own case for support. It should be developed and integrated with any existing cases for support with input from the board, staff leadership, and development office. This case for support is often written to convince the board and staff leadership that an endowment is important and worthy of dedicated resources.

The endowment's case for support explains where the organization stands today and what its aspirations are for the future. It explains how the endowment will make that future a reality. It describes why a substantial endowment is important, the kinds of gifts the endowment seeks, the gift vehicles available to donors, and the types of endowment funds that can be established. It also develops a time frame for the endowment's goals, describes methods of donor recognition, and suggests measurements for determining the success of the endowment program. It articulates what will be expected of members of the board. It does not describe the organization's needs. Donors do not care about the organization's needs; they care about the results, the outcomes.

The case for support will serve as the basis for developing a case statement, the basis of all marketing pieces aimed at targeted prospective donors. The case statement is discussed in Chapter 7.

The Case for Endowment Support

The process of developing the case for endowment support is more than a creative writing exercise; it also requires consensus building and often results in opportunities to cultivate prospects. The World YWCA had talked about building their endowment for a long time, but they had never written a formal case for support. When we helped them develop a formal case for endowment support, we found that the staff and governing board members had many different ideas about how the endowment might be used in the future. The process of reviewing and revising the case for support helped bring about a common vision for the endowment funds—and led more than one woman to consider including the World YWCA in her estate plan.

—Laura MacDonald, president of Benefactors Counsel in Columbus

Taking the time and expending the effort to develop the case for support at the beginning of the Endowment Action Program will pay big dividends in the long run. It will develop ownership in the program from those involved, and it will make sure that the organization has a clear understanding of what the endowment is intended to accomplish and why that is important.

The Structure of the Endowment Fundraising Program

The priority that the organization attaches to the endowment is made clear by the ways it takes advantage of existing fundraising programs and/or provides additional avenues of support to build the endowment. The organization has a variety of fundraising methods available to establish and build endowment assets, as detailed in the following sections.

TIPS & TECHNIQUES

Roles of Board Members and Colleagues in Endowment Building

The success of the endowment building program depends on how well the development officer can include other people in the work of building the endowment. Endowment building cannot be done by a person who is isolated from the board, the CEO, and other staff members, successful endowment building is a team effort. In organizations that have only one staff member with multiple responsibilities, that person must work closely with the board and advisors to launch the endowment building effort.

The **board of directors** provides essential leadership and direction for the formation of the endowment building program, approves appropriate gift acceptance and investment policies, allocates needed operating funds for the endowment program and staff training, and reviews periodic reports about its progress and performance. In addition, each board member makes a personal commitment to (1) make a financial investment in the endowment; (2) introduce friends and colleagues who are passionate about your organization to you or the executive director; and (3) participate in the program in other ways such as hosting a "house party," introducing professional advisors to your organization, soliciting gifts, or accompanying the development officer on calls to prospective donors.

The **executive director** is responsible for monitoring the creation and implementation of the Endowment Action Plan. The vision and committed support of the executive director focuses the work of board and staff members on endowment building strategies and encourages their ongoing work.

The **chief financial officer** manages the stewardship of the funds and works with the development officer and board committees to draft policies and agreements for the board's approval. Members of the finance staff prepare investment performance reports for committees, the board,

CONTINUED

59

TIPS & TECHNIQUES (CONTINUED)

donors, reporting authorities, and the annual report. The chief financial officer may meet with donors and their advisors about investment vehicles, spending policies, and drafting of gift agreements.

Other members of the **development staff** can be terrific allies. By working together on preliminary strategic plans for the endowment building program, they will understand the ways in which they can support the endowment building efforts, find common objectives and budget needs, and identify volunteers and prospective endowment donors. Members of the development staff need to be careful not to work at cross-purposes with one another. Remember to share the credit with your colleagues.

Marketing and communications professionals must understand the need for consistent and clear messages about the endowment to various constituencies. The messages are delivered through annual reports, newsletters, Web sites, brochures, advertisements, and even through the organization's program staff. Service providers and program directors who have direct contact with clients, patients, visitors, patrons, and others deal with people who may become prospective donors of endowment gifts in the future. Accordingly, everyone on the staff needs to understand the scope of the endowment program. You never know who will be the next person to make a significant gift to your institution.

Component of the Organization's Comprehensive Development Plan

Organizations that are serious about building endowment funds usually allocate resources to the endowment effort within the organization's comprehensive development plan. If the endowment is ignored or brushed aside in the organization's comprehensive development plan, neither the board nor the staff is encouraged to work for its growth. If there are competing tasks to be completed and goals to be met, staff members will focus their work on the areas that have been identified as priorities and on which their job performances will be measured. For these reasons, it is critically important to fully integrate the Endowment Action Program into all fundraising programs and activities.

Capital Campaigns with Endowment Components

Capital campaigns that involve bricks-and-mortar projects are especially appropriate to include endowment components, because prospective donors can readily understand the importance of providing financial stability for the long-term maintenance and upkeep of new facilities. Sometimes, the combined capital and endowment campaign makes the campaign for a facility more viable

IN THE REAL WORLD

Link Endowment Building to Capital Campaigns

Linking endowment with a capital campaign can be a wise strategic decision, as an Episcopal Diocese in the Midwest learned when it conducted an assessment before launching an $8 million campaign. Nearly everyone who had been interviewed identified John, a prominent and presumably wealthy church member, as a prime candidate to chair the campaign. But when John was approached, he declined, explaining that he couldn't make the anticipated $1 million lead gift and therefore felt that his leadership would be ineffective. When John learned that he could fund a portion of his gift with an irrevocable deferred gift, he gladly accepted the role of campaign chair and provided effective leadership. A campaign pledge that blends current support with a deferred gift is possible when the capital campaign goal includes endowment gifts.

—Laura MacDonald, Benefactors Counsel in Columbus

and convinces the donor that the organization has a plan to operate the new building. Capital campaigns may include policies that establish set percentages (perhaps 10%) of all capital gifts to be added to a quasi-endowment established by the board. Others seek donors who will direct their gifts to a permanent endowment for the benefit of specific facilities. The most common practice is to ask for unrestricted gifts to the permanent endowment, from which the board can allocate future distributions to the areas of greatest need.

Endowment Campaign

A general- or specific-purpose endowment campaign can be a successful way to reach a particular financial benchmark or jump-start a new endowment. An endowment campaign is similar to other capital campaigns but relies more heavily on one-to-one meetings and small group interactions. A well-designed endowment campaign includes concrete ways to continue building the endowment after the endowment campaign ends.

Special Gifts Campaign

Endowment funds for specific purposes lend themselves to special mini-campaigns within a larger program. Examples include higher education class endowment funds (50th anniversary class endowments are particularly popular), endowment funds to honor retiring staff or board members, and scholarship endowment funds, perhaps named in honor or in memory of a specific person.

Other Contribution Strategies

In addition to the aforementioned campaigns, fundraising strategies can be employed to increase endowment assets. Two are described as follows with their advantages and disadvantages:

The Story of Launching
One Endowment Campaign

The Yellow Springs Senior Center (YSSC) appointed a strategic planning committee to develop a five-year plan. As the committee considered the current and proposed programs that it wanted to offer, the committee decided that YSSC needed an endowment fund to protect its existing programs from financial risks before it added new programs. The YSSC launched a focused, one-year endowment campaign with a goal of raising gifts and commitments of $500,000 within the first year and a long-term goal of $1 million. They hired me to help them design a program to reach their goals.

As I write this, eight months into the year, $440,000 has been given or pledged to support YSSC in the future, and the public phase has just been launched. The board has strongly supported the campaign. The chair of the strategic planning committee and former dean of faculty at Antioch College, Connie Pelekoudas, has become the chair of the Endowment Campaign, and he has worked tirelessly to coordinate the work of committee members and to arrange face-to-face visits with current and former board members, current and former donors, and influential community members. Four board members and one former board member have conducted more than 50 personal visits in eight months. Others have developed marketing materials, including brochures, a video, campaign packets, and a Web site. Committee members have given presentations to local civic and social groups. Others planned a campaign kickoff party honoring people who were instrumental in supporting the organization during its 50-year history. The staff—all part-time employees—oversee direct mailings to nearly every home in their small community and track all gifts, which are deposited in a YSSC endowment fund at the Yellow Springs Community Foundation.

CONTINUED

IN THE REAL WORLD (CONTINUED)

Behind the scenes, policies have been established, a Legacy Society has been formed to recognize deferred gift donors, planned giving materials and training are under way, and systems to carry on endowment building programs in the future are being put in place. The board and the committee are excited about the campaign and fully understand the importance of continuing the program in the future.

1. *Earmark proceeds from specific special events for the endowment.* This method to raise additional endowment funds often uses a great deal of volunteer energy and time with limited financial benefit. Special events are usually more successful at introducing prospective donors to the organization rather than developing large contributions. On the other hand, if the event is financially successful, the endowment will receive an addition to its principal.

2. *Adopt a board policy to transfer a percentage of annual fund receipts into the endowment.* This method is not effective at encouraging large gifts from the donor's assets, but it does ensure that the endowment will continue to grow as long as the annual fundraising campaign is healthy.

Develop the Written Endowment Action Program

Board members, executive directors, and development professionals at non-profit organizations should design written Endowment Action Programs that will generate significant endowment assets over time and that are within the capabilities of the organizations' board and staff members to implement. The board and staff build the Action Program on information gathered in the fundraising assessment (described in Chapter 2). It includes a time frame (preferably five years) with goals, measurable objectives, and an estimate of the number of gifts and the size of gifts needed to reach the asset goal. In addition, the following information should be included in the Endowment Action Program:

- Gift options available to donors (Chapter 1)

- Endowment champions and committee structure (Chapter 2)

- Endowment case for support (Chapter 3)

- Structure of the endowment fundraising program (Chapter 3)

- Categories of prospective donors to the endowment fund (Chapter 4)

- Methods to attract, approach, and cultivate prospective donors (Chapter 4)

- Asking for and closing the gift (Chapter 4)

- Management of endowment assets (Chapter 5)

- Recognition and stewardship of donors and prospective donors (Chapter 6)

- Marketing the endowment (Chapter 7)

- Budget and staffing (Chapter 8)

- Evaluation of Endowment Action Program (Chapter 8)

The development of the written Endowment Action Program may seem like a daunting process for organizations that are new to endowment building, but don't falter. Take heart! The beginning plans may start out as a simple chart of planned activities. It is a living document that will be expanded and amended annually. Exhibit 3.1 demonstrates a sample format. Each organization should develop its own content and format for its Endowment Action Program.

A written Endowment Action Program provides a road map for the board and staff to follow in growing the endowment for an extended period. At the end of that time, the endowment will not be finished. Endowment building is an ongoing process, and the Action Program will need to be evaluated and updated regularly, but the most difficult part of the process is getting the

Example of an Endowment Action Program, Chart Format

Exhibit 3.1 shows a simple chart that organizations with a small development staff might use to explain and track strategies in their Endowment Action Programs. The chart can be expanded as the endowment building program grows. The person or persons responsible, the time frame, and the goal for each activity can be added to the chart. Some development officers track accomplishments in bold type right on the chart.

endowment started or reinvigorated. After the policies are in place, strategies selected, and activities consistently underway, the Action Program will help build a pipeline of planned gifts that will eventually be added to the endowment's principal. This growing pool of invested assets will produce an annual stream of income, permitting the organization to continue its good work in lean times and increase its programs and services when circumstances are favorable.

Staffing and Budget

When organizations begin building endowments, the staff responsibility is often added to the job description of existing development officers who already have too much to do. Sometimes, the executive director is the only staff member.

Not surprisingly, more and better-trained staff members are able to visit with more prospective donors and attract more gifts to the endowment. Thus, organizations that have decided to establish endowments should strive to initially dedicate one full-time person to this work—or, at a minimum, one-half

Example of Endowment
Action Program, Chart Format

Any Charity, Inc.
(year) Endowment Action Program
Goals for the year:

- Personal prospect visits: 24

- Number of gifts: 3 named funds; many smaller gifts

- New dollars: $100,000

- Board participation: 100%; board goal of $25,000 in gifts received

- New expectancies: $200,000

- Long-range goal: Assets of $_____ by the year_____

Donor identification and cultivation	Marketing	Special events	Professional advisor contact
Develop a list of 100 prospects through research and referrals	Send press releases about all endowment gifts, with the donor's permission	Host informal lunches for 4 small groups of current donors	Host a breakfast meeting of the board members' professional advisors
Identify contact person for each prospect	Develop a case statement and related materials	At the annual meeting, host a special reception for major and endowment donors	Ask prospective donors to include professional advisors in meetings
Train 5 volunteers to seek visits and accompany staff	Include articles about the endowment in the annual report and newsletter	Host a lunch for members of the press	Speak to groups at law and accounting firms
Schedule and complete 2 personal visits per month	Add pages to the Web site about the endowment		Contact known professional advisors to discuss endowment
Establish a Legacy Society	Send a mailing to donors who have contributed for 10 years or more		

of a full-time development officer's efforts. As the endowment building program and the endowment grows, additional staff members will be required.

Development officers focused on endowment building need both technical and people skills. Although both sets of skills are important, the technical aspects of the job can be learned, whereas relationship-building skills are often intuitive.

In addition to the development officer, a portion of the president's time will be spent with prospective donors, a financial officer's expertise will be required for investment and accounting matters, and marketing expertise will be needed as well. In addition, a substantial portion of an administrative assistant's work is required for data entry, marketing efforts, tracking and acknowledging gifts and pledges, and recognition activities. Personnel expenses will also include appropriate benefits and the cost of annual staff training.

There will be other expenses as well, although many of them may already be included in the development department's budget. For example, fundraising events, print materials and postage, office supplies, and donor tracking software and annual maintenance fees may have been budgeted for the organization's current fundraising activities, and only modest additions will be required for the addition of the endowment building program. Other endowment building strategies—such as the development of a comprehensive planned giving effort or upgrading the Web site to include planned giving vehicles and endowment options—may entail more substantial expenses, especially initially. Outside consulting services may also be required.

The initial expenses to begin an endowment building program may seem prohibitive, but the return on investment (the rate of gifts and expectancies for the endowment as compared with the cost to raise the gifts) over the next five to ten years is usually impressive. See Chapter 8 for information about measuring the cost per dollar raised and committed for the future.

Where Do We Go from Here

After the Endowment Action Plan has been drafted and everyone understands the case for endowment support, it is time to focus on identifying, cultivating, and soliciting prospective donors. Chapter 4 describes ways to (1) identify people who are likely to consider investing in the endowment and match their values to the values in the organization's mission; (2) cultivate prospective donors' interest, support, and commitment; and (3) propose gift solutions for donors' consideration, overcome objections, and close the gift.

Identifying, Cultivating, and Soliciting Prospective Donors

After reading this chapter, you will be able to

- Identify prospective endowment donors.
- Determine motives and blockages from the donor's perspective.
- Discover the intersection of the donor's values and the organization's mission and goals.
- Select cultivation and solicitation strategies that fit the organization's culture.
- Secure face-to-face appointments with prospective donors.
- Plan and execute visits with prospects and their advisors.
- Handle objections and close the gift.

Tell me and I'll forget; show me and I may remember; involve me and I'll understand.

—Chinese Proverb

To ask is no sin and to be refused is no calamity.

—Russian Proverb

Endowment fundraising, perhaps more than other types of fundraising, is about people. Donors give to charitable organizations because people need help or because people's lives will be enriched. Nonprofit organizations offer solutions to the problems and challenges people face. An endowment helps organizations that directly respond to people to continue to do so in the future.

Endowment donors are usually people—individuals and families—as opposed to corporations, businesses, or foundations. By carefully identifying and cultivating people who are prospective donors, organizations greatly increase the likelihood of receiving significant endowment gifts.

Before we delve into this topic, it is important to clarify the role of the organization's representatives (the CEO, development officer, or board member) with regard to the prospective donor. In this book, the organization's representative is usually referred to as the "development officer," although it could be a volunteer or another staff member. The development officer is not selling a gift or gift plan, manipulating someone to do what is best for the charity, or pushing the person into decisions. Rather, the development officer and the prospective donor together are "codirecting an interest and a desire to invest in something of value and encouraging the growth of that interest."[1] The development officer is an advocate for solutions to issues addressed by the organization that match the interests and values of the prospective donor. More about the topic of values is discussed later in this chapter.

One of the most important tasks of the board members is to tell prospective donors about their own gifts to the endowment and why they chose the specific type of gift or gift vehicle. The prospective donor will appreciate the board member's candor and clearly understand the level of the volunteer's commitment. Of course, this kind of personal testimony is possible only when the board member has already made a commitment and is willing to describe it.

Larger endowment gifts are usually planned gifts—those completed in concert with the donor's long-term charitable, financial, and estate plans. Planned giving programs are generally not broad-based fundraising efforts. More often, planned giving programs are designed for selected prospective donors. Thus, the multitude of potential prospects must be pared down to those with whom endowment building efforts are likely to be effective and productive.

Those seeking to generate gifts to endowment must understand the broad range of motivations for giving—and the reasons some donors do *not* give to endowment. The more the development officer knows about a prospective donor's life and motivations, the greater the chance of achieving positive results. Considerable research and listening may be required to determine each individual's relationship to the organization, family situation, financial ability, mix of owned assets, and even the donor's other charitable interests.

Don't hesitate to include other charities when talking about a gift plan with a donor. "The more life problems you solve for the donor with the gift plan, the greater the likelihood of realizing a gift from the donor," says Mike O'Sullivan, senior vice president for development at Children's Hospital Foundation of Columbus. "Don't just focus on your organization—focus on the total picture from the donor's perspective."

The development officer should suggest that others—spouses, children, other family members, professional advisors, spiritual advisors—be invited into the gift planning process. The prospective donor should be encouraged to include trusted allies at meetings. The development officer will thus have a chance to answer these allies' questions and concerns directly and understand their role in helping the prospective donor make decisions about the gift.

Concepts and strategies that work with prospective endowment donors are often different from those that are effective in annual fund and capital campaigns. Because the average planned gift takes two years to complete and more than three years to actually receive, organizations must focus their time and energy on those prospects who are most likely to give.

The cultivation of individuals and families for endowment gifts relies heavily on personal relationships and face-to-face visits. In order to build relationships based on trust and respect, the organization's development officer, often with a board member, needs to sit down with prospective donors to explore their values and charitable dreams.

Identifying Prospective Endowment Donors

Donors who make planned gifts are nearly always financially secure, which is not to say wealthy. They are highly acculturated into the American way of life and involved in a community that is larger than their own families. They visualize solutions to intractable problems and identify with organizations that provide opportunities for many people, rather than with specific needs or the needy. They seek organizations with which they share interests and values as partners to help them realize their visions for a better community or world. They decide to invest in a preferred future. Paul Schervish says that such donors, at least those who are wealthy, have "an inclination to be producers rather than simply supporters of philanthropic projects."[2] Clearly, the development officer needs to identify and cultivate these individuals.

Start Close to Home

Donors who contribute to the endowment are generally the people who are closest to the organization. They are:

- Current and former board members
- Current and former committee members and other volunteers
- Current and former contributors—annual and deferred—who are not in one of the previous categories
- Current and former clients, patrons, alumni, members, patients, family members, and staff

Because of their intimate involvement with the organization and their knowledge of its strengths and challenges, these individuals are most likely to understand the value of an endowment to the organization and to its ability to continue serving its constituencies. These individuals are most likely to commit their hard-earned assets to support the organization's future. Prospective donor referrals from people in these groups are also excellent prospective donors.

Profiles of Endowment Donors

In addition to affiliation with and knowledge about your organization, some groups of people are more likely to give to endowment than others.

- *People age 60 and older.* People who are retired or considering retirement are usually past the period in their lives when they are accumulating assets and building their estates. They have taken care of their responsibilities to raise and educate their children.

    People nearing retirement often have the greatest amount of capital to use for significant planned gifts, and tax advantages may be important to them. If they have not yet retired, they may have reached the highest level of earned income and therefore the greatest use for the income-tax charitable deduction generated by planned gifts. If they are retired, they may want the increased income possible from some planned gifts.

    Elderly donors may appreciate freedom from investment decisions. As people age, many will consider the legacy they will leave at their death, how they want to be remembered. This encourages donors to make significant gifts that will last in perpetuity.

- *Ages 50 to 59 and earlier.* In their peak earning years, donors are often focused on accumulating assets and paying expenses such as college tuition for children, mortgages, and the like. This, however, is the time to cultivate their interest in the organization by involving them as annual fund donors, volunteers, and board members.

- *Family situation*. Couples or individuals with no children, people whose children have independent wealth, and individuals with no close family ties are all prospects for endowment gifts. People in these circumstances often want to leave a legacy in their communities that will last beyond their lifetimes.

- *Past giving records*. Those who already support the organization— regardless of the amount—are likely to be interested in the organization's endowment. Those who have been consistent long-term donors are often better planned giving prospects, than are those who gave fewer but larger gifts.

  Donors who have notified the development officer of a planned gift to the organization (bequest, annuity, trust, and so forth) are likely to make a second planned gift. They may also increase and accelerate their commitments as family circumstances change and confidence in the organization grows.

  Family members of deceased donors, especially deceased donors who made planned gifts to the organization, have strong ties to your organization, and have seen the evidence of what charitable gifts can achieve. This is especially true where the deceased donor involved family members at the time the planned gift was negotiated with the organization.

- *Ethnicity and culture*. The ethnic and cultural backgrounds of donors are known to have an impact on their willingness to discuss and participate in endowment programs. The response of African Americans, Asian Americans, Latinos, Native Americans, and Europeans differ greatly over discussions of death and money. Talk of death and dying is seen by people in many cultures as tantamount to bad luck. Others find the subject simply rude and inappropriate and in conflict with their sense of obligations to family.

  Although all of these groups should be included in endowment work, development officers who identify and cultivate diverse prospective donors need to be sensitive to the differing cultural values of those prospects. This interesting and challenging subject of cultural diversity among donors is the focus of *Opening Doors: Pathways to Diverse Donors*, written by the author and published in 2002.[3]

- *Ability to give.* Individuals and families with significant assets are best able to make sizable endowment gifts and enjoy the tax benefits that accompany such gifts. Sometimes, people with significant assets are not easy to spot. Many have modest and private lifestyles, aptly described in *The Millionaire Next Door*.[4] They are conservative and responsible and expect the same from charities of interest to them. If charitably inclined, they make excellent prospects for endowment gifts.

Determining Motives and Blockages

The motivation for endowment gifts as well as the resistance to such gifts may be different for endowment donors than for annual or major gift donors.

Motivations of Endowment Donors

Motivations of endowment donors vary greatly and include the following:

- Passion for the mission
- Desire to make a difference
- Give something back
- Leave a legacy
- Belief in the work of the organization
- Confidence in the person asking for the gift
- Perpetuate an annual gift
- Dedication to the specific program that the endowment will fund
- Extend values to future generations, immortality
- Receive recognition in perpetuity

- Honor the past

- Ensure the future

- Promote the organization's self-sufficiency

- Ensure perpetuation of values regardless of leadership in the future

- Keep the organization focused regardless of fads

- Assure involvement with peers

- Continue family history with the organization

- Provide income for oneself and/or others

- Belong to a worthwhile organization

- Simplify life

- Lessen tax burden

- Set example of philanthropic giving

The challenge for the development officer is to discover the motivation of individual prospective donors, even when the prospects may not be consciously aware of what drives their own charitable giving. Often, people's values, morals, and ethics determine that which motivates them to make major charitable contributions (see the later discussion on Discovering Shared Values).

Reasons Donors Resist Giving to Endowment

It is important to be aware of the reasons that donors resist making gifts to endowments, including the following:

- Insufficient passion for the cause

- Lack of confidence in the organization or its leadership.

- Lack of confidence in the long-term future of the organization

- Fear of organizational complacency

- Absence of immediate gratification

- Fear of future financial insecurity

- Loss of control

Some of the reasons that a prospect might say "no" are directly related to the development officer's work. If these error opportunities are anticipated, they can possibly be avoided:

- Asking too early, under asking, not asking

- Asking for the wrong program

- Asking by the wrong person

- Not listening to the prospect

- Making it hard to say "yes"

- Surprising the prospect

- Failing to follow up promptly or as requested

- Failing to show respect

- Assuming too much about the prospect's interests or values

- Inadequate preparation

- Failing to sell a dream

Incorporating the Gift into Estate and Financial Plans

As evident from the previous discussion, the decisions of prospective donors are influenced by a variety of factors—personal, philanthropic, spiritual, psychological, practical, emotional, and financial. All of these considerations are valid. Many of these factors can be addressed by incorporating the decision about the endowment gift into the donor's overall estate and financial plans. A holistic approach facilitates discussion about taxes, estate planning, and charitable goals with the donor, the donor's family and advisors, and with representatives of the organization. These conversations can move a reluctant prospective donor to review priorities, assets, and estate plans and to consider a significant gift for a lasting purpose. Although tax savings are usually not the reasons for gifts, tax savings may permit larger gifts or earlier gifts than otherwise anticipated.

Cultivation and Solicitation Strategies

Discovering Shared Values

Major gifts, including endowment gifts, occur at the intersection of the donor's values and the organization's mission and goals.

The organization's development officer, often with a volunteer board member, must discover the prospective donor's significant interests and core values. "The job of the development director," says Doug Allinger, president of Allinger and Company, Inc., in Columbus, "is to make the linkage between the principles or qualities that the donor finds to be intrinsically valuable and the organization's priorities and work." The development officer must connect the part of the organization's work that affirms the donor's values.

This linkage, this connection, can only happen in face-to-face visits with individuals, couples, or families. Thus, the visits with donors should focus on the donors' values and how the donors can extend their values beyond their lifetimes through gifts to the endowment.

Face-to-Face Visits

Initial Contact

The initial contact with the prospective donor may be a letter or a phone call. The person who establishes the initial visit (the board member or the development officer) probably has his or her own preference. The initial contact, like

TIPS & TECHNIQUES

A Letter of Introduction

The letter of introduction should include information about:

- Who you are
- What you are doing
- What you want
- What you will do

SAMPLE:

Dear Elizabeth:

You have been a friend of Our Charity for several years, and I want you to know how much we appreciate your involvement. You and I met briefly at the auction last year, shortly after I started as Our Charity's development officer.

I'm writing at the suggestion of our mutual friend, Bill Donor, who speaks very highly of you. Bill is an active member of our board, and he tells me that you are a committed volunteer for Our Charity. I would like to have the opportunity to visit with you for 45 minutes or so. We are in the process of establishing a permanent endowment for Our Charity, and I would like your reaction to our preliminary plans to launch our endowment building effort.

While it is my hope that you may ultimately consider a gift to Our Charity, my only request at this time is that you share a few minutes with me to discuss the benefits we will offer donors and our plans for the endowment's growth.

I will call you within the next few days to arrange a time when we can meet. Meanwhile, thank you very much for your interest in Our Charity.

Sincerely,

P.S. Bill said that I should ask you to tell me what originally motivated you to become involved with Our Charity.

all contacts with donors, should be personal and warm. Tell the prospective donors why the contact is being made and that their relationship to the organization is appreciated.

The initial contact, whether by phone or letter, to set up the personal visit should be made by the person who is most likely to succeed in getting an appointment. This is best done by a board member who personally knows the prospective donor. If there is no such board member, work to find a personal link to the donor, someone who will be able to arrange the meeting.

The call, like the letter, is short and to the point:

"We're calling a few people to ask for advice as we prepare to launch an effort to build our endowment. Can we visit with you next week?"

This kind of approach tells the prospective donor:

- The organization thinks that the prospective donor's support is important.

- The organization wants the prospect's advice.

- The organization is preparing to start an endowment building program.

The selection of a date for the visit immediately moves the conversation from the theoretical to the practical. If the prospective donor cannot meet the next week, select another date. The goal is to establish a face-to-face meeting at a quiet location. It could take place at the prospective donor's home or office, at the organization's facilities, or at a neutral location such as a restaurant.

"We would love to have you come for lunch in the board room here at the Daycare Center, or we could come to your home, or we could meet at the Riverside Grille on Main Street."

Offering options allows the prospective donor to make a choice without having to explain the reasons for the choice. The goal is to make it both convenient and comfortable for the prospective donor.

Be persistent in your phone call; do not take a single "no" for an answer. Many substantial gifts have been made after an absolute and unequivocal "no"

TIPS & TECHNIQUES

First Impressions

The old saw "you only have one chance to make a first impression" is certainly true with visits to prospective donors. Here are some simple tips that may already be obvious to you:

- Do your research about the prospect and practice your opening remarks, primarily so that you don't talk too much during the first visit.

- Dress professionally and appropriate to the prospect's lifestyle.

- Arrive on time. This lets the prospect know that you take your work seriously and that you can be counted on.

- As you walk to the front door, put a smile on your face and stand up straight.

- Hold your notebook in your left hand so that you will be able to shake hands with your right hand.

- Greet the prospective donor using the appropriate title and last name, unless he or she has already told you to use a first name. This approach may seem formal to you, but it will demonstrate respect and politeness. Of course, if the prospect requests that you use his or her first name, by all means do so.

Now that you have set the stage with a positive first impression, an open and productive conversation is likely to follow.

to the first cultivation effort. However, respect the prospective donor's answer. If "no" is the answer, express thanks and move on.

Before the Visit

Send the prospective donor a reminder letter of the date and time of the visit and a brief reference to the endowment program. Be certain that it is sent in a timely manner. The letter is stronger if it comes under the signature of the board member who arranged the meeting, but the development officer may send it if the board member is unable to do so.

Before the first visit, the development officer, with input from the board member, should prepare a written purpose statement indicating the objectives for the first visit. The purpose statement should reflect the primary development goal, which is to match the values and donative intent of the prospective donor with the organization's priorities and work. Limit the first meeting to attainable goals, such as the following:

- Tell the prospective donor about the organization's priorities and work and about the endowment building program.

- Learn about the prospective donor's values and involvement with the organization.

- Answer any questions the donor may have about the organization and its endowment.

In preparation for the first visit, the development director should ask the board member to be prepared at the meeting to share his or her commitment to the endowment. If the volunteer has not made a commitment (heaven forbid!), then the development officer should be prepared to share one or more stories about gifts that have been given to the endowment. The development officer should practice describing the organization's priorities and work in a few sentences, and draft a list of probing, open-ended questions about family, work, charitable interests, and so forth to take along on the visit (see Tips & Techniques).

Consider publications that might be appropriate to take along on the visit. Gather materials such as the annual report, newspaper clippings about a current program, or perhaps a testimonial from a satisfied client or customer. Don't take so much reading material that the prospective donor will be overwhelmed or that the organization will have nothing of interest to send later. It is often most effective to give the prospective donor the materials to review at the close of the visit.

TIPS & TECHNIQUES

Asking Questions
of Prospective Donors

Before a visit with a prospective donor, write down several open-ended questions that can get the conversation going and uncover those things that give meaning to the donor's life. This is not to suggest that you plow through a list of questions or a personal inventory with the donor. You want the prospective donor to share information and values, not feel put on the spot or the subject of an inquisition. Do not become so attached to your preselected questions that you neglect to follow the conversational lead of the prospective donor. A picture of personal information and core values will emerge as the relationship with the donor develops.

Appendix B contains a list of introduction questions and questions to be asked at subsequent visits. The sample questions can be interwoven into a variety of casual conversations or can be structured in face-to-face visits over time.

The First Visit

The first visit is a visit, not an interview or interrogation. Like all visits, it begins with brief chitchat. Remember, however, that the visit is scheduled for 45 minutes only. As soon as practical, the person who arranged the meeting—usually the board member—should tell about his or her involvement with the organization and state the purpose of the visit. The development officer should outline the mission and work of the organization and do so in five minutes or less. The tone should be warm, but concise and direct. The actual time for this beginning will depend both on the development officer's organizational skills and on the extent of the questions and participation by the prospective donor during the opening remarks.

After explaining the work and priorities of the organization, it is time to move the conversation in a direction that begins to connect that work and those priorities to the values of the prospective donor. Ask an open-ended question about the donor's interest and prior experience with the organization. Now listen. Really listen. Empathize with the donor's personal interests, circumstances, and goals. Take notes. Listen for clues about the person's motivations, such as the following:

- Values of importance

- Passion about a particular program

- Desire to see that certain causes continue

- Interest in increased income

- Tax avoidance

See the previous discussion about Motives of Endowment Donors in this chapter for additional examples.

Also at the first meeting, present the case for the endowment and describe the organization's program to increase the endowment's size and impact. Share ways in which the endowment will build the organization's capacity, ameliorate the uncertainty of other funding sources, provide increased financial flexibility, and permit the staff to creatively serve clients in the future. Adapt your presentation to each person's unique situation. Convey a sense of urgency. Listen for questions and interests. Discuss common concerns and find common ground. Match the prospective donor's interests with the organization's programs that impact people.

Determine the prospective donor's interest in further contact—another meeting, a visit to the facility, a meeting with a professor doing particular research, or information about planned giving techniques. At the end of each visit, establish a firm date for the next meeting. Try to arrange a specific task to be accomplished by both the staff member and the prospective donor for the next visit: "I will find out the answer to your question about hummingbird research and give it to you at our meeting in November, and you will locate a copy of the life insurance policy we talked about." Close the visit by thanking the prospective donor for his or her time.

After the Visit

As soon as the organization's representatives and the prospective donor part company, the development officer and the volunteer should sit down on the nearest park bench or pull into a coffee shop to record the visit and establish the next action steps. The staff member takes written notes, on a notebook computer or a legal pad, so that information and the essence of the meeting will be systematically captured. Always write notes as if the prospective donors are likely to review them—this avoids any embarrassment later. Write down each promise made to the donor and the date your work is due. The donor wants an answer to the hummingbird research question, and the answer is due at the November meeting.

When the staff member returns to the office, the electronic database should be updated promptly. The process for handling information must be routine and fail safe in order to ensure that the information is available to other staff or board members who may meet with the prospective donor in the future. In order to prevent unauthorized use of personal information, the database should be accessible to selected people only.

Send a thank-you note immediately. A handwritten note is always appreciated. If the visit included personal information and family history, send a copy of your notes for editing, correction, and verification by the prospective donor. People will often add more information to your biographical sketch to ensure that your records are accurate and complete.

Schedule the follow-up plans, by adding action steps to the calendar and preparing relevant materials. If others need to become involved, get them scheduled now.

TIPS & TECHNIQUES

People Usually Enjoy Sharing Their Own Stories

I first started in the fundraising business in the early 1980s at the Ohio Historical Society. I would begin nearly every visit with prospective donors by asking about their family's history. I asked questions such as, "How long has your family been in Ohio?" "Where did you grow up?" "What was it like?" The conversation usually moved to current employment, volunteer commitments, and current family members. In subsequent visits, I learned more about the prospective donor's accomplishments, hopes, and values, especially as they related to the Society's mission to protect and promote Ohio's rich history.

I always brought along a notebook and took lots of notes. After each visit, I would type them up and send them back for corrections and additions to the prospect with a personal note of thanks for meeting with me. I told the prospective donors that I wanted to be sure that I had accurately recorded our conversation, because the corrected copy would be permanently retained in the Society's archives.

"Why would they want to keep information about my family?" they would sometimes ask.

"When the Society receives your planned gift years from now," I would answer, "people will want to know about the person with the foresight to provide a lasting legacy for future generations." The Society's prospective donors appreciated that their stories would not be lost to time.

During the past two decades of visits with potential philanthropists for many organizations—in diverse fields such as community foundations, education, social services, the arts, and health care—I have found that nearly all people want their stories to be heard and taken seriously. And they want to achieve their personal philanthropic dreams and learn about effective ways to make a lasting difference to their communities.

Continue the relationship until the next scheduled meeting through any of a variety of cultivation techniques such as sending newspaper clippings, providing written tax and financial information, involving the prospective donor with the institution, enlisting other members of the staff or volunteers to assist with cultivation, or simply calling to say "hello." See Chapter 6 for more ideas about follow-up with donors.

IN THE REAL WORLD

A Lesson in Making the Ask

Mr. Jackson* attended our senior lunches every Friday and was a regular at the monthly Lunch and Learn Lecture Series. As the development director, I attended many of these programs to get to know the seniors and have them get to know me, to talk about giving, and to quietly teach creative charitable gifting methods one-on-one in a nonthreatening environment.

The director of the senior program pulled me aside one day and told me that Mr. Jackson had mentioned more than once that he had "a substantial amount designated for our organization in his will." She thought I might want to know this, and I did!

I asked the director if she would be willing to meet with Mr. Jackson and me to talk about the possibility of making a gift in memory of his wife, who I knew had died recently. The director agreed. We talked about the organization, the programs he attended, and his wife. I asked him if he would consider establishing a named endowment fund in her memory. He was extremely touched and said he would consider my suggestion.

When he asked how much it would "cost," I told him that to endow the Lunch and Learn Lecture Series in her name would require a contribution

CONTINUED

IN THE REAL WORLD (CONTINUED)

of $100,000. He sat back and said that was a lot of money. I told him that he could make an outright gift or set up a gift through his will (he was more than 80 years old). He told me that he would speak with his attorney and get back to me. I found out after he left that the "substantial amount of money" he had designated for us was $5,000. Obviously, the amount I mentioned to him was quite a shock.

Thirty minutes later, I was sitting in my office still writing up notes from our visit when Mr. Jackson called. He was ready to endow the program in his and his wife's name for $100,000. He thanked me for the opportunity to memorialize his wife and to leave his own legacy at our organization.

Six years later, I am with a different organization, but I still smile when I receive the notices about the Estelle and Sam Jackson* Lunch and Learn Lecture Series.

*Names have been changed.

—Susan Axelrod, a planned giving consultant in Rexford, New York

Subsequent Visits

Subsequent visits may include both the board member and the development officer or the development officer alone, as appropriate. Continue to write down objectives for each visit. In the course of several visits, the following questions should be answered:

- What are the prospective donor's primary interests and values?

- What is the prospective donor's history with the organization?

- Would the individual like to have additional information about the organization and its endowment program? If so, what would be most helpful?

- Are any programs, facilities, or other facts about the organization of special interest to the individual?

- What are the prospective donor's personal and family circumstances and goals?

- What are the individual's philanthropic and legacy goals?

- Is this person receptive to thoughts of supporting the endowment program? If not, in what other programs is the prospective donor interested?

- Has the individual considered including the organization in a will or trust? Is the organization already in the will?

- Did any specific planned gift technique seem of particular interest to the prospective donor?

- Should other individuals, such as the CEO or board chair, visit with the person?

When most of these questions have been answered, it is time to develop a charitable plan that addresses the prospective donor's basic motivations (see the previous Motives of Endowment Donors section in this chapter). These motivations can be grouped into four primary categories:

1. *Values.* Providing support for the most important things in life, making important programs permanent, paying back a debt to those who have gone before, and so forth

2. *Ego.* Appeal to personal pride, need for self-approval or approval of others, fear of losing face, and more

3. *Financial.* Fear of loss of control, need for security, reduction of taxes, maximize inheritance of heirs, and others

4. *Satisfaction.* Feeling of accomplishment, sense of pleasure in providing for others, desire for immortality, and the joy of making a lasting gift to the future

TIPS & TECHNIQUES

More Cultivation and Solicitation Ideas

Additional thoughts about cultivation and solicitation include the following:

- *Always* keep in mind the importance of confidentiality.

- Be prepared to change strategies—to annual giving, capital projects, and so forth—if the prospective donor's interests do not match the endowment.

- Take advantage of the unique opportunity to use words such as *permanent, legacy, perpetuity,* and *forever* when discussing endowment gifts.

- Seek advice and experience as needed from legal counsel and financial specialists; bringing in relevant expertise demonstrates maturity and trustworthiness.

- Involve the family. Cultivate and recognize all family members and suggest that the fund be named for the family rather than an individual or couple, so that future generations might add to it.

- Accept rejection. No organization receives contributions from every prospective donor. Yet even individuals who have not made a gift may spread the news of the organization's excellent programs and attract support from their friends and colleagues.

Develop and Present the Gift Proposal for Consideration

The development officer should draft a gift proposal for the donor's consideration. The proposal should tie together the donor's long-term goals and interests with the work and priorities of the organization. Present the gift proposal for consideration in person, using a cost-benefit approach. In the draft, explain the following:

- How the gift will be used by the organization

- How the gift works

- An approximate gift amount

- The type of assets that might be used

- Tax implications of the gift

- A target date to complete the gift arrangement

Ask the prospective donor to participate in something significant. Donors are usually flattered by requests for large gifts and can always counter with a smaller dollar amount. Watch the prospective donor's reaction and respond accordingly. Ask for gifts that are significant enough to justify the staff and volunteer time.

If the gift will establish a named endowment fund, prepare draft language for the gift agreement. See Chapter 7 for additional suggestions for drafting the agreement.

Always encourage the active participation of the individual's legal and financial advisors, as well as family members (spouse, children, or others), in every meeting.

Many donors and their families are involved in and passionate about several charitable organizations. Do not view other organizations as competition. Instead, consider them partners in helping your prospective donors accomplish their philanthropic goals. Work with the development officers at the other organizations to present a comprehensive giving plan that incorporates all of the donor's interests.

Overcoming Objections

Prospective donors usually ask tough questions and express concerns before they commit to investing significant amounts in an endowment. The first step is to make sure that the concern has been correctly understood. Second, offer a clear and complete response to the concern.

IN THE REAL WORLD

You Are Not a Legal or Tax Advisor

Your role is to connect the donor's values and charitable goals with suggestions for ways to structure meaningful gifts. You help donors explore their options and you may prepare gift illustrations, but you always explain that you do not give legal or tax advice—even if you are trained as an attorney, accountant, or financial planner. Because you work for the nonprofit organization, your advice would not be independent, and every donor should be encouraged to obtain independent professional advice.

As standard practice, tell prospective donors—both orally and in writing—that you and your organization do not provide legal or financial advice and that you strongly recommend that they seek independent advice from their own professional advisors. Include such a disclaimer on all cover letters, gift illustrations, and brochures.

Objection: Your goal for the endowment sounds awfully high.

Response: It sounds like you're wondering why we need that amount of endowment to get the impact we've talked about. Am I correct? (pause) The reason is...

Objection: I don't believe in endowments. I want to see what my money buys.

Response: Perhaps you'd like to know specifically how the net earnings of your gift would be used. Would that address your concern? (pause) Here's how the endowment makes a powerful and specific impact on the people we serve...

Objection: We are overcommitted.

TIPS & TECHNIQUES

Ethical Solicitations

You and your organization have a basic duty of care toward your donors. This means handling every donor contact with integrity and honesty. Your ultimate goal is not just to close the gift, but to build a lifelong relationship between the donor and your [organization].

Planned giving [and giving to endowment] works well only when the donor feels fully satisfied with his or her gift experience. Make sure you disclose every significant aspect of the gift arrangement, so your donor has no unexpected surprises. Think about how you would want your mother treated, and treat your donors the same way.

—John Elbare of Florida Philanthropic Advisors in Lutz, FL, "Five Tips for Safe Solicitation" in *Planned Giving Mentor*, June 2004.

Response: It sounds like you would like to invest in our organization, but can't see how you might do that right now. Am I right about that? (pause) Would it be helpful if I explained some of the ways others have managed this problem? (pause) They...

Try to anticipate objections from the prospective donors and deal with them immediately. Once the concern or question is clear, offer one or more potential solutions.

After a concern has been stated and answered, move past that issue. Try this technique: "I know you are concerned about _____. If that were not an issue, what would you like to accomplish with a gift to the endowment?"

Other prospective donors seem to waffle when asked for a commitment. Sometimes it helps to try to clarify their indecision. For example:

Noncommittal: Let me think about it and I'll get back to you.

Response: What factors will you consider as you weigh our proposal?

Closing the Gift and Following Up

After the preliminary gift proposal has been fine-tuned, prepare a second draft for the prospective donor's approval.

Practice closing techniques in advance (see Tips & Techniques). Rephrase, in summary fashion, the opportunity, benefits, shared values, and the expected gift. The job of the development officer is to help people understand what must be done and give them the opportunity to experience the magical joy of doing it.

TIPS & TECHNIQUES

Techniques for Closing the Gift

Practice various approaches to closing gifts—with colleagues, in front of the mirror, or at home with your spouse. Different prospective donors require different techniques. As you will discover, practice makes this critically important task less uncomfortable. With all techniques, remember to focus on the dream and the people who will benefit.

- *Leadership close.* "As an important leader in this community and in this organization, your leadership gift to the endowment is important."

- *Minor point close.* "As we finalize your gift, let me be sure that I understand the name you want. Is it The James Johnston Fund or The James Johnston Family Fund?"

- *Review of benefits close.* "Let's review what this gift will mean to you and to the organization. You will receive income from the trust for the rest of your life as well as a current income tax deduction in the year the trust is funded. The organization will..."

- *Close with the mission and vision.* "We envision a day when every child and every woman lives in a safe home. In order to make that vision a reality, we want to increase our intervention and educational services for nearly four thousand children next year—and that requires a significant endowment..."

IN THE REAL WORLD

Donors Are the Best Prospects

During a one-on-one interview with a board member and recent endowment donor to a local women's foundation, I asked her opinion of the foundation's fundraising practices.

"We have a dedicated cadre of volunteers in an organized annual fund program," she said. "But this year they did not include me in the annual fund drive. I am appalled! I was ready to increase my annual gift, since I've now made such a major commitment to The Women's Foundation. But no one asked me for a gift."

At the closing of the gift, especially for a significant gift, the organization may want to plan a short ceremony. This is an opportunity for the CEO, board chair, chief financial officer, and development director to thank, acknowledge, and congratulate the donor and greet the family. Significant gifts deserve significant attention. Respond to the occasion with appropriate thanks and attention. Remember to take photographs for the organization's newsletter and the local newspaper.

Keep or place endowment donors on the prospect list for annual and capital campaign gifts. Their endowment gifts are not necessarily the only gift they will make this year, and they are likely to want to continue their annual support in the future.

Where Do We Go from Here?

The identification, cultivation, and solicitation of prospective donors was addressed in this chapter. The broad variety of charitable motivations was discussed, as well as how to uncover the values and priorities of prospective donors. Techniques for effective face-to-face visits with prospective donors were described, including ways to handle objections and close the gift.

TIPS & TECHNIQUES

A No Does Not Mean Not Ever

Sometimes, even with the best preparation, you can get "no" for a response. Some very good fundraisers—professionals and volunteers—consider a 50% to 60% "yes" rate a high level of success.

Furthermore, it is very important to understand that a "no" often isn't what it seems to be. It can mean no to this ask, but not another amount; not now, but "yes" at a later date; or "no" to this project, but not another.

—Doug Allinger, president of Allinger and Company, Inc., in Columbus

The responsible management of the funds is integral to the stewardship of the gift and the future cultivation of additional gifts. The next chapter covers investment of the assets and options for managing the endowment. The various policies and procedures appropriate for an Endowment Policy Manual are described.

Notes

1. Barbara R. Diehl, JD, and Robert Finley, CFRE. "Putting the Gift in Gift Planning: The Philosophy and Practicality of Donor Cultivation and Stewardship." 14th National Conference on Planned Giving, 2001.

2. Paul Schervish. *Major Donors, Major Motives: The People and Purposes Behind Major Gifts.* Boston: Social Welfare Research Institute, Boston College, 1997, p. 31.

3. Diana S. Newman. *Opening Doors: Pathways to Diverse Donors*. San Francisco: Jossey-Bass, 2002.

4. Thomas J. Stanley and William D. Danko. *The Millionaire Next Door*. Atlanta, GA: Longstreet Press, 1996.

CHAPTER 5

Managing, Investing, and Establishing Policies

After reading this chapter, you will be able to

- Understand the three factors that determine the growth of endowments.
- Choose an appropriate structure for the management of endowment assets.
- Select and monitor investment managers.
- Establish an endowment policy manual.
- Explain investment and spending policies.
- Design acceptance policies for endowment gifts.
- Develop draft gift agreements.
- Establish fund documentation and gift administration practices.

Giving should be entered into in just the same careful way as investing. . . giving is investing.

—John D. Rockefeller

T he prudent supervision of the assets in the endowment is one of the most important responsibilities of the board of directors. This duty is often referred to as *stewardship*: "the careful and responsible management of something entrusted to one's care."[1] When an organization receives its tax-exempt status under state and federal laws, the board of directors becomes publicly accountable for stewardship of the organization's resources, including its endowment.

As discussed in Chapter 1, true endowments are established by endowment gifts from donors; quasi-endowments are established by the transfer of the organization's assets by the board of directors; and term endowments are established by either donors or boards for a set period of time. For all three kinds of endowments, their growth in the future is determined by three factors:

1. *Additional gifts.* New endowment gifts increase the size of the capital assets, which, in turn, produce greater earnings. Usually, donors of endowment contributions have been cultivated over a period of time to develop their trust in the organization, deep understanding of the organization's purposes and programs, and excitement about its future to make outright or deferred endowment gifts. The staff, board members, and endowment committee members are usually charged with designing and carrying out strategies to fully equip donors to make informed decisions about endowment gifts. These concepts and strategies were discussed in Chapter 4. For quasi-endowments, the board may regularly or periodically transfer funds to its endowment.

2. *Return on investments.* Endowment assets also increase with good investment results. A long-term investment objective for most endowment funds is to provide a stable and consistent level of program support, in perpetuity. To accomplish this objective, endowments seek to maximize the purchasing power of the assets so they will keep pace with inflation over time and provide revenue to the organization. This requires an investment policy that spells out the endowment's goals and diversified investment strategies.

3. *Spending policies.* The third factor in growing the purchasing power of the endowment is the amount distributed to programs by the endowment.

This amount is often called the *net assets released*. Because the endowment's primary purpose is support of the organization's programs, boards of trustees are tempted to distribute (spend) the endowment's earnings. Such practices, however, can cause dramatic fluctuations in program support. The old practice of distributing the endowment's "earnings" or "income" has been replaced by carefully crafted spending policies that balance the growth of the corpus and distributions for current programs.

However, an especially cautious board may be tempted to hoard the funds in the endowment and not distribute anything for fear that a rainy day may come. This discourages donors who, after all, gave their gifts with the expectation that they would be used to make a difference, not merely sit untouched in the endowment.

This chapter deals with the latter two factors, the return on investments and spending policies. It describes options available to the board of directors for carrying out its financial stewardship of the assets entrusted to its care and other policy issues that need to be discussed and resolved.

Providing Responsible Investment Management

The skills and experience required for the management of endowment assets are different from those needed to oversee operating funds and reserve accounts. Organizations need to analyze the structures and options available to the board of directors regarding its endowment investment policy and management of the endowment's assets on an ongoing basis. The three endowment management structures most commonly used by nonprofit organizations are (1) internal, (2) affiliated foundation, and (3) community foundation.

Internal

Many organizations manage and administer their own endowments. The endowment program, both attracting gifts to the endowment and managing the endowment's investment, should be fully integrated into the organization's development and finance functions. The development office raises funds for the endowment as well as for annual operations, special programs, and capital expenses. The development office also keeps current information about and builds long-term relationships with endowment donors. The business office oversees the financial aspects of gift valuation and disposition; makes investment decisions based on the organization's investment and spending policies; sends accurate and timely payments to planned gift beneficiaries and prepares tax forms for beneficiaries; and prepares periodic reports to the donors, beneficiaries, and the board of directors. Some aspects of this work may be managed in-house, and others may be overseen by the finance office with the day-to-day work assigned to an outside manager such as a bank, trust company, or brokerage firm.

The benefits of keeping the management and administration of the endowment internal to the organization include cost savings, accountability, and simplicity. As the endowment grows and the planned giving program develops, these tasks can become daunting for small and midsized organizations. When this happens, it may be time to turn to outside investment management and administration. (See the later section on Selecting and Monitoring Investment Managers.)

The organization may want to use outside endowment management and fundraising consultants when starting an endowment program or reinvigorating a languishing program to provide expertise and focus. It is essential to have access to legal counsel that is experienced in planned giving, because various legal issues will arise as the program grows.

Affiliated Foundation

Some nonprofit organizations establish separate 501(c)(3) affiliates [supporting organizations, as defined in Section 509(a)(3) in the Internal Revenue Code], which are commonly called *foundations*. These are popular with nonprofit organizations that receive substantial governmental funding (e.g., hospitals);

produce a sizable portion of their revenue from earned income (e.g., universities); or are governmental agencies (e.g., the county children's center or the local library board). These foundations have their own boards of directors with separate bylaws, articles of incorporation, investment policies, and operational practices. Their board members usually are appointed in part or entirely by the supported (parent) organization.

Sometimes the foundation is the fundraising arm for the parent organization and sometimes its sole responsibility is to manage endowed assets for the benefit of the parent organization. The decision should be made early on if the foundation board will ultimately raise funds, because that decision will affect the job description for board members and the people who are asked to serve. The parent organization's board is likely to think that it no longer needs to raise funds if the foundation's board is assigned to that task.

Once the foundation board is fully functioning in a fundraising role, however, the parent organization's board can focus on programs and service delivery. It may have limited interest or expertise in fundraising. A separate entity with a board of directors dedicated to raising and managing funds can be an effective ally. The foundation permits the organization to identify and recruit community power brokers to the foundation's board with the necessary clout and stature to attract significant endowment gifts. The foundation's board is also charged with managing the endowment and overseeing its administration, freeing up the organization's board to focus on the vision and guidance required to accomplish the organization's mission.

Many national nonprofit organizations have established supporting organizations to manage endowments and planned gift vehicles (such as gift annuities and pooled income funds) for their local chapters or affiliates. They usually hold greater assets than any one affiliate and can command better rates of return at lower costs than any individual affiliate could do on its own. The local chapters retain the task of attracting new contributions, and the supporting organization administers the assets.

IN THE REAL WORLD

Remain True to the Donor's Intention

Although separate foundations can be practical, care must be taken to ensure that the foundation and organization remain inextricably linked. A zoo in the Midwest discovered the importance of this constraint when its foundation began to make unilateral decisions about the release of endowment assets, including some distributions to unrelated conservation organizations, even though the donors intended the assets to benefit the zoo.

Community Foundation

Community foundations—operating in more than 700 communities in the United States and in more than 350 communities around the globe[2]—offer another alternative. Through separate component funds called *organizational* (or *agency*) *endowments funds*, local community foundations oversee the investment of the fund's capital and distribute a portion of the fund's year-end value back to the organization at least annually.

As an example, the Anytown Jazz Band (AJB) received a windfall endowment gift of $150,000 from the estate of a 20-year season ticket-holder. The AJB board decided to use the gift to establish the Anytown Jazz Band Endowment Fund at the Anytown Community Foundation (the Foundation). AJB irrevocably gave the Foundation the $150,000 to establish its permanent fund. The Foundation will make annual distributions to AJB subject to its spending rate, which is currently 5% of the endowment's value. The Foundation charges a small fee for its services in administering the fund.

The benefits to AJB in establishing an organizational endowment fund at the community foundation include the following:

- The foundation's board is experienced in endowment fund management, thus freeing up AJB's board to focus on the organization's mission and programs.

- The investment choices and the potential for a better return on investment increase with a larger investment pool.

- The community foundation will process gifts to the AJB Endowment and may accept types of gifts that AJB would not accept on its own, such as real estate or closely held stock.

- Acknowledgment letters that meet IRS requirements are provided by the community foundation to every donor to the AJB Endowment Fund. Of course, AJB will want to personally thank donors as well.

- The community foundation's investment oversight may provide additional credibility and comfort to AJB's donors.

- The community foundation will list AJB's endowments in its annual report and offer planned giving technical assistance to AJB and its donors.

- If AJB ceases to exist in the future, its fund will remain at the community foundation and will benefit another organization whose mission and purposes are similar to that of AJB.

Before an organization launches an endowment building program, it needs to carefully decide which structure it will use to manage its assets and adopt the necessary policies and procedures to responsibly carry out its duties.

Selecting and Monitoring Investment Managers

Organizations may serve as their own investment managers. As these organizations begin to build their endowments, many do not have the money to attract the interest of institutional investment managers and endowment administrators. Many corporate fiduciaries require a six- or seven-figure minimum account, which excludes small and growing endowments from outside professional management. Generally, small organizations have small staffs with little experience in and little time for administering planned gifts or managing an investment portfolio.

These small organizations often limit the kinds of gifts they accept and the types of gift vehicles they offer to accommodate their limited staff size and expertise. This may reduce the likelihood that some prospective donors will make contributions. Some financial institutions offer investment management services to local nonprofits as a public service, so don't fail to ask. In *The Complete Guide to Planned Giving*,[3] Debra Aston provides thorough guidance about selecting outside managers and developing a Request for Proposal for planned giving services.

Each endowment fund has its own purpose. Likewise, it should have its own set of investment objectives. Lynda S. Moerschbaecher, in *Building An Endowment Right from the Start*, states:

> The investment managers who actually implement the investment management and are charged with meeting the investment objective must also understand the stated purpose of the endowment fund(s). Every fund held by an institution may have a different need for income versus growth, timing of distributions, and risk/reward.[4]

The board of directors should assign responsibility for reviewing management and custody of the endowment to a specific group, perhaps a joint subcommittee of the finance and development committees. In the contract with the investment manager, include a formal investment review, the benchmarks against which performance will be measured, evaluation of the performance at least annually, and procedures to modify or end the relationship. Steven L. Mourning's comprehensive article, "What Development Officers Need to Know About Investment Performance," provides background about investment performance, why and when investment returns are important to development officers, the balance of risk and return over time, and considerations in measuring and reporting performance.[5]

Developing an Endowment Policy Manual

An Endowment Fund Policy Manual, created to ensure financial integrity, should include all of the policies related to the endowment and all of the procedures for its administration. The manual should be reviewed and updated regularly to reflect changes in laws and regulations.

Written Policies Are Critically Important

Written policies are important to secure the trust and confidence of board and staff members, prospective donors, and professional advisors. Most policies will be used as both an internal guide and an external cultivation document. They are documents to be shared with donors and their advisors. Policies should state that the organization is prepared to accept gifts other than cash and publicly traded securities, define the kinds of gifts that are acceptable, and explain the process for giving and accepting such gifts. The policies should provide guidance for development staff and volunteers and help professional advisors assist their clients in making appropriate gifts effectively.

Responsible policies demonstrate that the board takes its fiscal responsibilities seriously and that the organization is professional and trustworthy. Credibility takes years to build and, once lost, could take even more years to regain. Written policies protect the organization and its board of directors from their own and the staff's mistakes and ignorance. Policies help protect the organization and members of its board from well-meaning donors who want to establish endowment funds for purposes that are not part of the organization's mission or in ways that may be detrimental to the individual or the organization. Increasingly, sophisticated prospective donors expect to be able to review the organization's gift policies before making investments in its future.

TIPS & TECHNIQUES

Standards of Practice

In addition to board-adopted policies specific to your organization, consider adopting general practice standards such as those included in the National Committee for Planned Giving's *Model Standards of Practice for the Charitable Gift Planner* and the Association of Fundraising Professionals' *Donor Bill of Rights*. Both documents are included in the Appendixes.

Finally, the development of written policies offers the opportunity to help board members understand various gift arrangements and the implications of accepting certain types of gifts. As board members become more familiar with the process of endowment building, many will begin to identify how they or their colleagues might participate as donors.

Endowment policies should be reviewed at least annually and revised as necessary.

Investment and Spending Policies

Organizations that have chosen to manage their own endowment assets need to develop investment and spending policies to guide the endowment managers.

Definitions

Two terms related to investment policies are important for the development officer to understand:

1. *Total return.* A measurement of overall investment growth that includes earned income (dividends and interest) plus realized and unrealized changes in the market value (gains and losses)

2. *Net assets released.* The portion of endowment value used for current operating needs or specific programs, usually determined by a three- to

five-year moving average of the endowment's value multiplied by a pre-specified board-approved percentage, referred to as the *spending rate* or *endowment withdrawal rate*.

See Chapter 8 for endowment projections using these concepts.

Developing an Investment and Spending Policy

An investment policy outlines the organization's investment objectives and tolerance for risk. For example, it might specify what percentage of the endowment will be invested in equities and what percentage in fixed-income instruments. It might prohibit certain equity investments, such as commodities and real estate, require socially responsible investing, and require a minimum rating for fixed-income investments. It might establish specific benchmarks that the investment return should meet or exceed.

The matters of investment and spending are interrelated. The organization will want to keep the net assets released at or within levels that will permit the corpus of the endowment to remain intact over time. Sample investment and spending policies from the Council on Foundations' Community Foundation Fundamentals Course are included in the Appendixes. They will provide the organization with a starting pointing in the development of its own investment and spending policies.

Debra Ashton offers this explanation of spending policies:

> To manage an endowed fund program, the trustees of a nonprofit organization establish a spending limit for endowed funds based on a percentage of the fund's value, usually on the first day of the fiscal year. This spending limit changes over time, but it is tied to the concept of investing for a total return on the assets. There is no tax on short-term or long-term capital gain for a nonprofit organization. Therefore, while the endowment investment objective is for total return including income and capital appreciation, a separate spending rate allows for reasonable use of the donors' funds while allowing excess income or appreciation to stay in the fund so that the principal can keep up with inflation.[6]

The investment and spending policies should also address administrative fees to manage the endowment. Will each fund be assessed a portion of the costs, or will the organization bear the costs in its own operating budget? There is no right or wrong answer, but any fees associated with endowment funds should be clearly explained in writing so that no later misunderstanding occurs about the way the endowment funds are being managed.

Most boards of directors assign the drafting of the investment and spending policies to their finance committees, which present the policies to the board for full discussion and approval. As an alternative, an endowment management team—composed of board members, representatives from the business and development offices, together with financial and legal advisors—is often an effective group to develop such policies. The adopted policies are shared with the investment manager(s), interested prospective donors, and their advisors.

Acceptance Policies for Endowment Gifts

Acceptance policies for endowment gifts protect the interests of both the endowment donors and the organization. Everyone involved in the gift process—prospective donors, staff and volunteers, and professional advisors—should know what gifts can be accepted routinely, what gifts require approval by the board, and what gifts are generally not accepted.

Donors of charitable gifts must assign a value to their gifts to establish their charitable income tax deduction. The tax regulations relating to valuations of charitable gifts are complex, and tax deductions depend on how and when the donor acquired the asset, its current value, and the organization's use of the gift. Gift acceptance policies help avoid misunderstandings or conflicts between the donor and the organization about gift valuation and processing. In addition, policies can encourage boards of directors to use windfall gifts to build the principal in its quasi-endowment. Every organization engaged in an endowment building program needs such policies.

The policies should include the following:

- Kinds of endowment gifts that the organization accepts

- Purposes for which endowment gifts are accepted

- The minimum gift size and other standards for establishing a named endowment fund

- Processes involved in gift acceptance and administration

- The authority of staff to negotiate and accept gifts and when the board or a committee must review and approve gift arrangements

- Substantiation and disposition of gifts, including a provision allowing the board to place unrestricted memorial gifts and planned gifts into the Endowment Fund

- Circumstances under which a financial valuation amount will or will not be acknowledged to the donor in the acknowledgement letter

- Methods by which the acceptance policies for endowment gifts are regularly reviewed and may be amended or changed

Sample acceptance policies for endowment gifts are included in the Appendixes.

These policies are basic and do not include comprehensive policies for complex gifts, such as life insurance, real estate, or closely held stock. A review of the sample policies is a worthwhile part of a thoughtful process of organizational self-examination. Each individual organization should establish the types of gifts it will accept, the limit on conditions attached to those gifts, and which gifts they have the resources and willingness to manage.

Special fiduciary responsibilities apply to gifts that create irrevocable life income arrangements. Before accepting management of these types of gifts, check with the organization's legal and financial advisors.

Gift Agreements

Gift agreements define the terms of understanding with the donor, which are particularly important with endowment gifts. Some gift agreements are implied based on the written or oral promotional materials of the organization, such as special events advertised as: "All proceeds from this concert will be added to the YWCA's Endowment for Racial Equality" or "Your ticket to the Scholarship Banquet helps support the University's Scholarship Endowment." Gifts in response to written materials seeking gifts for endowment are also considered to have been given by implied agreement. These are considered gifts to true endowment.

Larger endowment gifts, however, should be accompanied by a written gift agreement that articulates the donor's intent and the organization's commitment to carry out that intent. Endowment donors and their families often have considerable influence in the community, and disgruntled donors have been known to report their dissatisfaction to the Attorney General or the news media. No organization wants this kind of notoriety. See Tips & Techniques for a sample endowment agreement.

The development officer who drafts the gift agreement must be trained to consider the long-term nature of endowment gifts and the challenges in drafting contractual documents that will be binding on the organization as circumstances change in the future.

Recognition Policies

Recognition policies should be adopted to provide a standard for donor recognition. Endowment donors should generally be covered under the organization's general donor recognition policies. However, endowment donors may expect and deserve additional recognition beyond annual and major gift donors. See Chapter 6 for suggestions and ideas.

Endowment Fund Documentation

Gifts to endowment must be carefully documented and that documentation safeguarded for the protection of the donor and the organization. The Uniform

Sample Bare-Bones
Named Endowment Agreement

The Fred and Thelma Smith Endowment Fund at One Charity, Inc.

This agreement between Fred and Thelma Smith and One Charity, Inc. establishes the Fred and Thelma Smith Endowment Fund (the Fund). Fred and Thelma Smith have delivered a check in the amount of $_____ to One Charity, Inc., to establish the Fund.

I. One Charity, Inc. shall make distributions from the Fund to be used for its charitable, educational, and public purposes in accordance with One Charity, Inc.'s Investment and Spending Policy adopted by its Board of Directors. [The donor may wish to restrict the use of the distributions to specific programs or areas of work.]

II. One Charity, Inc. agrees to:

a. Invest and manage the Fund in a manner consistent with the Investment and Spending Policy adopted by the Board of Directors. Endowment funds are pooled for investment purposes.

b. Hold and preserve the Fund as a permanent endowment fund for the purpose(s) outlined above. However, if the purpose for which the endowment distributions are restricted should cease to exist or become impossible or impractical to carry out, the Board of Directors reserves the right to direct distributions from the Fund to such other purpose or purposes as it determines to be consistent with the donors' original purpose as described above.

This agreement is made on _____. (date)

By _____ _____
    Fred Smith   Thelma Smith

By _____
    President of One Charity, Inc.

CONTINUED

TIPS & TECHNIQUES (CONTINUED)

[This sample is presented for illustration purposes only. It does not constitute legal advice. Each organization should ask an experienced attorney to review and draft its named endowment agreement. When drafting an agreement for a particular gift, add information about the donor and the donor's family. Be clear about any restrictions or designations on the use of the distributions from the fund.]

Management of Institutional Funds Act (UMIFA) requires this documentation. Chapter 1 described the three types of endowments: true endowment, quasi-endowment, and term endowment. The organization is required to track these three types separately, although it is permitted to commingle the funds for investment purposes. Thus, each endowment gift to principal should be categorized by type.

In addition, the development office should keep a file—often both electronic and on paper—for each major endowment donor. The file should include the following information:

- Donor profile

- All correspondence to and from the donor

- Contact reports

- Information from advisors

- History of gifts to the organization

- Pledges

- Planned gifts

- Endowment gift history with date, amount (fair-market value on date of delivery), type of gift, purpose of gift, restrictions on gift and gift agreements, if any

- Copies of transaction documents
- Endowment fund description

Endowment fund descriptions for named endowments must be carefully documented because the board of directors is responsible for carrying out the terms of the gift both now and in the future. Some of the issues that must be included in the endowment fund description are as follows:

- The name of the fund

- Full name of the donor(s) with address(es)

- Listing of the assets transferred to the fund for outright gifts and planned gift arrangements for testamentary transfers

- Donor restrictions on the use of the fund

- If the fund is established for competitive purposes, such as scholarships or faculty awards, provide a description of the donor's selection priorities. Remember that the donor may be involved in an advisory capacity only; recipients are chosen by the organization or a panel it establishes.

- Provisions regarding future additions to the fund by the donor, family members, or the general public

- Signatures of all parties, including the president of the organization

- Donor recognition commitments

Many organizations prepare a draft fund agreement in a donor's name as a persuasive tool used to cultivate prospective donors who have expressed interest in an endowment gift.

"One of the most effective marketing tools in planned giving is the fund description. A personalized fund description is an excellent means of encouraging a donor to consider giving at a higher level to a fund established in the donor's name or in the name of a loved one," state Ronald R. Jordan and Katelyn L. Quynn in *Planned Giving: Management, Marketing and the Law*.[7]

Their book offers sample endowment fund agreement forms and describes the mechanics of a fund description.

Endowment fund documentation is especially important for endowment and planned giving donors because it often takes years to complete a gift, and staff members may change over that period of time. In addition, research demonstrates that once a person has made a planned gift, he or she is more likely to make another one in the future.

Gift Administration

The administration of the gift must function efficiently and in compliance with the terms of the gift agreement. Appropriate procedures and safeguards must be in place and functioning. This may mean assisting with the transfer and valuation of assets, seeing that appraisals are completed, and working with the banks and brokerage firms. If checks are to be received from donors to pay life insurance premiums, for example, someone needs to be sure that they are received in a timely manner and in the proper amount. The final gift documents must be prepared, mailed for signature, returned, and filed appropriately. These details make the difference between a satisfied donor, who is likely to consider additional gifts or make referrals to others, and an unhappy donor, who is unlikely to consider another gift and certain to tell others about the mistake.

Where Do We Go from Here?

The responsible stewardship of the endowment assets honors the donors' investments in the organization's future. The nurturing of relationships with donors, prospective donors, family members, and professional advisors takes sensitivity, careful planning, flawless follow-through, and appropriate recognition. These topics are covered in Chapter 6.

Notes

1. *Merriam-Webster's Collegiate Dictionary, 10th Edition*, Springfield, MA, p. 1150.

2. Eleanor W. Sacks, "2004 Community Foundation Global Status Report." Worldwide Initiative for Grantmaker Support—Community Foundations (WING-CF). Brussels, Belgium, 2004.

3. Debra Ashton. *The Complete Guide to Planned Giving: Everything You Need to Know to Compete Successfully for Major Gifts*, Revised Third Edition. Quincy, MA: Ashton Associates, 2004.

4. Lynda S. Moerschbaecher, with contributing authors Barbara G. Hammerman and James C. Soft. *Building an Endowment Right from the Start*. Chicago, IL: Precept Press, 2001.

5. Steven L. Mourning, "What Development Officers Need to Know About Investment Performance." *The Journal of Gift Planning*, National Committee on Planned Giving, Indianapolis, IN, 3rd Quarter, 2004.

6. Ashton, Ibid. p. 355.

7. Ronald Jordan and Katelyn Quynn. *Planned Giving: Marketing and the Law.* New York: John Wiley & Sons, Inc., 2000, p. 57.

CHAPTER 6

Caring for Donors and the People They Trust

After reading this chapter, you will be able to

- Understand the donor's expectations of accountability and recognition.
- Establish standards and mechanisms for donor services.
- Build relationships with legal and financial advisors.
- Acknowledge gifts and honor donors appropriately.
- Select effective recognition events and remembrances.
- Communicate with donors after gifts are complete.
- Customize special opportunities for selected donors.

I shall pass through this world but once. Any good therefore that I can do or any kindness that I can show to any human being, let me do it now. Let me not defer or neglect it, for I shall not pass this way again.

—Mohandas "Mahatma" Gandhi

Endowment donors have made investments in the long-term viability and growth of organizations that they trust and value. These donors have entrusted their philanthropic aspirations into the care and custody of charitable organizations. Chapter 5 described the organizations' obligations to wisely and thoughtfully invest, distribute, and manage the assets contributed to them. This chapter discusses the equally important service responsibilities to donors, prospective donors, their families, and their professional advisors. Such donor services begin with a philosophical commitment to accountability and meeting donor expectations. Donor services foster strong relationships between the nonprofit organization and the people who are committed to it.

Charitable giving involves an exchange relationship in which the donor has certain expectations of the organization. Endowment donors in particular may expect nonmonetary benefits such as courtesies and a continuing relationship. They have made gifts that will support organizations in perpetuity; the organizations, in exchange, have obligations to their donors for the long haul. Donor services include honoring the intent to make a gift, paying attention to the gift process, communicating with the donor after the gift is complete, and sustaining the relationship for the long-term benefit of both the organization and the donor.

Get It in Writing

Strategies to encourage constituents to increase their involvement with the organization as participants, volunteers, and contributors are important and integral components of the Endowment Action Program. The growth of endowment assets, discussed in Chapter 5, is directly tied to the addition of new gifts to the endowment. New gifts depend on personal, long-term relationships with donors and prospective donors—the very relationships that effective donor services enhance. Endowment building programs that successfully incorporate focused, thorough, and goal-oriented donor services programs continue to attract new and repeat donors.

Development officers must tailor the techniques of donor services to the organization's distinct constituency. Set goals and standards for the donor services program described later in this chapter. Develop ways to measure results of the donor services program and the staff's work, as discussed in Chapter 8. The staff is more likely to carry out the process of proving that the organization is worthy of the donor's continuing support if their work is recognized. Remember the axiom "you get the behavior that you reward."

In addition to including a structured program of donor services in the Endowment Action Program, the organization must provide the resources—people, time, and money—necessary to carry out the program. Donor services must become an organizational priority. The most likely endowment donor is one who has already made one or more gifts to the organization, especially a donor who has made gifts over many years.

If the organization does not already have one, it should establish or purchase a prospect and donor tracking software system, preferably one that is compatible with financial software already in use in the business office. Such a system should track personal information, family information, financial information, involvement with the organization, special interest areas, names of legal and financial advisors, and planned giving vehicles of interest. This information must be captured in writing, especially for endowment and planned giving prospects, because the cultivation of these donors may span the time and service of multiple development officers.

Response Mechanism for Inquiries

First Responder

Donor services begin with the prospective donor's first contact with the organization. Often a call or note comes in response to a pleasant or profitable experience with the organization, because of a new awareness of the organization's programs, or (more rarely) in response to a direct mail piece. The way that contact is handled often determines whether the organization will get the privilege of a visit with the donor. The staff person who fields such calls, often the receptionist, must be welcoming and informed about the organization. If the organization's telephone calls are answered by an electronic message, be sure that the caller is able to speak directly with a knowledgeable person with one selection and without having to listen to a long electronic recording.

Often the first responder will refer the call to another staff member. It is important that the referral is appropriately made, for example:

- "You will want to talk with Brian Smith, our volunteer coordinator. Let me connect you with him now."

- "Sally Johnson, our development director, will be able to give you all the information you need about that. Unfortunately, she is on another line just now. May I take a message or put you through to her voice mail?"

The critically important first impression may make the difference between developing a relationship with the prospective donor and never hearing from the prospective donor again, and *all* callers should be treated as prospective donors.

Response Mechanism for Endowment Inquiries

Develop a response protocol for all endowment inquiries that includes the following components:

- *Receipt of inquiry.* Once the call, e-mail, or letter has been received, establish a policy to follow up within 24 hours. This does not mean that the questions have to be answered in the organization's initial response, but the donor should be notified that the question has been heard and is being taken seriously. This lets the donor know that the organization recognizes that the inquiry is important and assures that the donor is contacted before he or she forgets that information was requested. A quick return e-mail or phone call is sufficient:

Building Trust Begins with the First Interaction

One donor told me that she wanted to make a $10,000 endowment gift, but she wasn't sure which organization she wanted to support. She sent inquiries to four organizations about their endowment programs. The first organization sent her a form letter in two weeks, with an enclosed brochure. The second organization sent her a personal letter three weeks later stating that they didn't have an endowment, but would be delighted to have an annual gift of that amount. The third one never responded. The fourth organization responded immediately with a personal letter asking for a meeting and followed up with a phone call the next week. Which one do you think actually received the gift?

○ "We have your request for more information and it will be in the mail on Friday."

○ "Thank you for the great questions. I'd like to check with our attorney before answering. I have an appointment with her on Thursday, and I will call you after that meeting."

○ "I have sent you one of our brochures in today's mail. I'll call next week to be sure you received it and to answer any additional questions you may have."

● *Answering questions.* Answer inquiries with a personal letter and appropriate information. Never send a form response or a brochure without a letter. If the inquiry is from a current or past donor, acknowledge that fact in your response. Let the person know that you will call within the week, and immediately schedule the phone call on your calendar.

- *Personal visit.* A face-to-face visit with the donor is the most valuable and important aspect of the cultivation process—whether cultivating for a first or a subsequent gift. The initial phone call and personal visit are discussed in Chapter 4. This is the most critical part of the donor cultivation process. Do not skip it. The process is a little like jumping off the diving board for the first time or learning to drive a car—it gets easier and more fun with practice. Take someone with experience, when appropriate, to discuss gift options with donors until the staff member develops technical expertise. Most donors will find this an indication of professionalism and respect for the donor's unique situation.

- *Make the process easy.* Make it easy to do business with the organization by having standard forms available to donors and their advisors, carefully preparing materials in advance, and offering to make any changes quickly. The development officer's job is to make the process of making an endowment gift as simple and effortless as possible for the donor, while explaining each step of the process and the implications of the transaction.

- *Build relationships with trusted advisors.* Be sure the prospective donor's legal and financial advisors are invited to appropriate activities and events. Ask some advisors to serve on the professional resource committee, to help select planned giving materials, to write an article for the newsletter, or to speak at a planned giving seminar. Provide them with the material and draft language to make their jobs easier and to help them serve their clients. Sometimes, the most trusted advisors are not in legal or financial professions, but rather ministers, family members, or mentors, so include them, too.

  Honor advisors who have helped complete gifts to the organization or who have provided professional expertise, perhaps by recognizing them at the annual meeting or on the organization's Web site. Prepare a list of experienced advisors to share with prospective donors who ask for referrals. Refer to Chapter 7 for information about marketing to advisors.

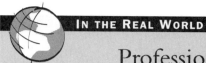

In the Real World

Professional Advisors Can Make or Break a Gift

When Barbara Zimmerman, senior gift planner for the Women's Foundation of Minnesota, gave a presentation on endowment building at the annual conference of the Women's Funding Network—a national consortium of women's funds—she spoke of the importance of advisors. She asked everyone who'd received an endowment gift via a professional advisor to raise her hand, and nearly every hand in the room went up. One fund reported that 80% of its planned gifts resulted from the fund's outreach to professional advisors.

Gift Acknowledgment

Always thank donors and acknowledge gifts promptly and appropriately.

Be certain that acknowledgment letters are neat and accurate and meet the IRS requirements for the type of gift received. Make sure that the names and addresses are correct, and get the salutation right. Don't jeopardize the next gift with sloppiness.

Individualize acknowledgment letters by confirming that what is expected will be done correctly. For example, if the gift is a memorial gift, state that the family has been notified of the gift, but not the amount. If there are restrictions on the gift, reiterate the restrictions and how the organization will carry them out. The donor must be confident that the organization understands and will honor the donor's intent for the gift.

Don't limit the donor gift acknowledgment to a written letter that complies with the IRS requirements. Give the donor something special, such as a thank-you visit, a phone call, or a handwritten note from the CEO or board chair—or both. In other words, don't let the donor's only acknowledgment be made through the standard channels used for $10 annual gifts. The form of the acknowledgment must match the importance of the gift to the donor and to the organization.

Expressions of genuine thanks are always appreciated. Daniel Conway explains the phenomenon in *Achieving Excellence in Fundraising*:

> Most nonprofit organizations readily accept their responsibility for gift acknowledgment, but there is a danger in seeing this as merely an administrative function routinely carried out by an efficient development office. Saying thank you—even in simple ways—is often the most profound opportunity an organization has to communicate with people who have freely chosen to share in its philanthropic mission. Gratitude is a powerful and engaging emotion. When it is expressed genuinely, from the heart, it creates a strong bond between the organization and the donor being thanked.[1]

Say thank you more than once. Let donors know that you have not forgotten them just because their gifts are completed. Keep donors involved with the organization. Happy donors often make subsequent gifts, and they speak to friends and relatives about their gifts, thereby opening possibilities for future gifts from donor referrals.

Donor Recognition

When donor recognition is considered, development professionals often think in terms of published donor lists, walls of honor in lobbies, and plaques for the donors' offices. Yet the most appreciated ways to honor donors are often simple and personal benefits, customized to the *donor's* needs and interests.

Use of Contribution

Communicate to donors how the distributions from their gifts are being used and who has benefited. Show how the donor's goals have been advanced by the gift. The development officers that accept the duty to keep endowment donors informed about the organization and how their gifts are being used are the most successful at attracting additional support. This kind of personal

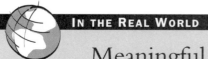

Meaningful Recognition from the Donor's Point of View

A recent widower and major donor to a Big Ten university retired to Florida before completing his gift to establish a faculty chair in the history department at his alma mater. After the gift was finalized, the development director sent him an acknowledgment letter, complete with the gift valuation and a statement that he had received nothing of significant value in return for his charitable gift. He also received a handwritten note from the chairman of the history department. He was satisfied with the recognition.

Several months after the completion of the gift, the donor received a letter from the president of the university stating that he would be vacationing nearby in February and inviting the donor to lunch during that week. The donor replied in writing that he would be honored to have lunch with the president, and asked if he could bring a friend with him since he no longer drove a car. Three days later, the donor received a phone call.

"The president wants to know if you would like to invite some friends to join you for lunch at the country club with him. There is a round table that can accommodate up to ten people, so invite whomever you like."

The donor invited eight people from his condominium association, some of whom had prior relationships with the university and some of whom didn't. The president greeted the donor as a good friend and, during lunch, told everyone about the innovative work of the new chair of the history department, made possible by the donor's gift. Lunch lasted for two hours, mostly recounting stories about college days in the 1940s. The president was delighted to learn about the earlier era, often asking for additional details. Since then, the donor made two more planned gifts to the university, and three others at that table have made significant gifts as well.

communication, directly related to the gift, is greatly appreciated and deepens the donor's relationship with the organization.

Appropriateness

Set standards for donor recognition, but remember that many endowment donors may "test the waters" with a small gift as they contemplate making a larger gift later. Show special appreciation for first-time gifts, while making sure that the show of appreciation is appropriate to the act. The president of a major university will not be able to have lunch with every $10,000 donor.

Special Opportunities

Personal interactions and connections are most appreciated—the more personal, the better. Betsy Mangone says that, in general, "stewardship is changing from a process of honoring and recognizing donors as a class, to honoring and recognizing donors as individuals."[2]

Offer special opportunities to donors to your organization. The options include lunch with the CEO or board chair, backstage tours, picnics with grantees, receptions with the speaker after a lecture, auditing a specific class, or program notes sent before the concert. Make personal introductions to staff members who may be of particular interest to the donor. One donor to the symphony was invited to sit in on auditions, for example. An architect, who had made a significant contribution to the school of architecture from which he graduated, was invited to listen to students' senior presentations.

Ask donors to submit an article for the organization's newsletter or magazine about a personal experience or their area of expertise. Ask donors to loan something to the organization—perhaps their home for an event or space in their offices for a meeting. The benefits that donors seem to like best are those that bring them closer to the organization.

IN THE REAL WORLD

Connect the Donor with Those Who Benefit from the Gift

A successful entrepreneur and graduate of a community college established a scholarship endowment at the college in 1999 for marketing students. As the donor discussed his goals for this scholarship with the development director, he stated that he wanted the criteria in selecting recipients to focus on hard work and perseverance rather than academic success or grade point average. The development director made sure that the donor's criteria were written into the scholarship agreement, and she attended the first meeting of the scholarship selection committee at the college to tell the committee about the donor and his stated criteria.

Each year, after the scholarship committee selects the recipients, the development officer writes to the donor with information about the students' backgrounds and interests. In May, an annual scholarship reception is held at the college, and the donor is invited to assist the dean of the marketing department in making the scholarship presentations. The donor, the recipients, and the recipients' families have the opportunity to meet in person. After the reception, the development officer sends the recipients the donor's contact information and suggests to the recipients that they may want to keep in contact with him. In the five years since the establishment of this scholarship fund, three significant additions have been made to it, and the donor has more than doubled his gifts to the annual fund.

Frequency

Recognition should be given frequently and in varied formats. Remember that the goal of recognition is to meet the donor's expectations. It is not recognition if the donor doesn't recognize it as such. Send cards or notes to donors on Thanksgiving, their birthdays, or the anniversary of their gifts. Send notes to donors when their names are in the paper or their children perform in the school play. Precede a mailing with a phone call, or follow the mailing with a phone call. Stay in touch by telephone or e-mail. Invite the donor to functions, events, activities, and annual meetings—all aimed at keeping the connections strong. Send newsletters, press releases, and newspaper articles about the organization. Take endowment donors to lunch at least annually. Add handwritten notes to form letters. Very few people object to being thanked or thought about too often. As Barbara Ciconte and Jeanne Jacob say in *Fundraising Basics*,[3] "It is best to err on the side of too much information than too little."

Gifts of Appreciation

Some donors feel strongly that they do not want more "stuff" in their lives. Be sensitive to their wishes. If you want to send a small token gift of thanks, make the gift something of high quality, not expensive, that will remind the donor of the institution.

 IN THE REAL WORLD

Build and Grow
Lasting Relationships

Doug Allinger, of Allinger and Company, Inc., in Columbus, consults with several retirement communities across the United States. He says that sometimes residents do not want to tell the development officer that they have completed their planned gifts because they enjoy the staff visits and want them to continue. One man told Doug: "Once the planned giving person knows about the gift, that's the last I'll see of her." How sad. Make sure that this is never said about your staff or your organization.

Public Recognition

Do not assume that everyone wants public recognition—ask the donor first. Some people will appreciate the thought, but not the attention that recognition can engender. People who do not want public recognition or who want to remain anonymous *do* want to be thanked in appropriate ways and, usually, to be involved with the organization. Just because the donor does not want to be recognized at a public luncheon does not mean that the donor doesn't want to be taken to lunch.

For donors who do not decline public recognition, list their names in the annual report or publish, both electronically and on paper, an annual Stewardship Report that summarizes the year's philanthropic record. Include profiles of donors and of the programs and clients that benefit from the endowment funds. A recognition plaque can be hung for a special endowment campaign, or one plaque can be used for all endowment donors, or one plaque can list all planned giving donors while identifying those who gave to the endowment.

Fund Updates

Prepare individualized reports for the donors of named endowment funds on the funds' current status at least annually. These reports should include the fair-market values, realized and unrealized gains or losses, fund earnings, distributions made, and gifts added. Also report on the use of the net assets released. Whose life was made better because of this fund? How was the quality of life in the community improved? If it is a scholarship fund, include biographies of the recipients. Evidence of the impact of their gifts is important information to donors.

The sending of fund reports offers an opportunity to make contact with endowment donors. Enclose a personal letter about new programs at the organization, recent research that has been undertaken at the organization, or changes in the organization's spending policies.

All endowment donors should receive an annual report on the status of the organization's endowment and the projects that it supports. This might be done by sending out the organization's annual report with a special cover letter highlighting the accomplishments of the endowment.

Recognition Groups and Events

Recognition groups and events are used for five primary purposes:

1. Publicly thank donors now for gifts that may not be received for many years in the future.

2. Encourage others to consider their own planned gifts to the organization.

3. Maintain contact with endowment and planned gift donors, thus increasing the likelihood that they consider additional gifts in the future.

4. Provide ongoing opportunities for donors and their family members to participate in the life of the organization.

5. Introduce donors to other donors who have made similar gifts.

Often, the recognition group will sponsor the event or events, but that is not required.

Recognition Groups

About Recognition Groups

If the organization does not have a heritage group or legacy society to recognize those who have made planned gifts to benefit the organization at a time in the future, the endowment building program can be the impetus to start one. If it does have a recognition group, consider separating the endowment donors into a special subgroup or clearly identifying them in listings of members.

Recognition groups can make endowment solicitation easier for some; it may be more comfortable to ask prospective donors to join the legacy society than to make a planned gift. Find an appropriate name for the recognition group, such as the name of an early pioneer, a recognizable aspect of the mission, or the importance of the members and their gifts. For example, the Alzheimer's Association of Central Ohio decided to call its recognition group the Forget-Me-Not Society. Consider offering a special status, such as "Founding Member" to those who accept membership within a specified period.

Qualifications for Membership

Sometimes organizations establish separate recognition groups for endowment donors, bequest donors, planned gift donors, and so forth. In organizations that are just entering endowment building and planned giving, one recognition group may make more practical sense. The group should be as inclusive as possible of people who have made commitments for future gifts. Verbal confirmation is generally accepted from the donor. Although some people could claim that they have made provisions when they have not, development professionals have found that most donors eventually give organizations much more than was expected or promised. Some organizations require a minimum size gift to qualify for the legacy society, whereas others believe that all planned gift donors should be included, knowing that planned gifts are usually the largest gifts that donors make.

Recognition Events

About the Events

Recognition events usually do not raise funds for the organization. They generate goodwill and support in the future. Be clear about the purpose of every event before its planning begins: to identify new prospects, cultivate existing prospects, or sustain relationships with those who have already given. Make sure that the planning team is clear about the purpose of the event—and that the total event supports that purpose. Invitees should include donors and family members, prospective donors, professional advisors, and other appropriate constituents. Staff members may be invited to talk about the ways in which their departments have benefited from the endowment. If possible, include individuals—such as scholarship or staff award recipients—who have benefited directly from the endowment. In advance, ask one or two of the donors to give personal testimonials about their gifts, what motivated them to make their gifts at this time, and how the gifts have enhanced their lives.

Planning for the Event

The planning of the event is an opportunity to involve donors and prospective donors. Remember the basics of event planning such as timing, geographic location, accessibility of facility, and ease of parking. Older people may have special limitations or needs. For example, some older people do not drive a car at night; others may be insecure in new environments. Keep careful records of planning and preparation for the event. It may become an annual tradition.

Event Follow-up

Be sure to capture the contact information for everyone who attends the event. Place them on the mailing list for future communications. Personal notes to donors and prospective donors in attendance from the CEO or board chair show people that their presence was important and appreciated. An alternative is to send each attendee a copy of the annual report with a personal note. If the prospective donor indicated a possible interest in a particular program or project, a personal note from an institutional leader involved with that program is appropriate. If you know the names and addresses of those who could not attend, a personal letter with a copy of the program or some other commemorative material demonstrates to the person that his or her absence was noted.

Special Prospects and Donors

Not all donors or prospective donors are equal. Some deserve and require special treatment.

Current and Former Board Members

Most current board members need education about the value of the endowment, the various vehicles available to them for making their gifts, and their responsibilities in relation to growing the endowment. Personal meetings, one-on-one, permit the board members to ask questions and focus the conversation on their own specific interests and allow the development officer to thank each board member personally, listen carefully for each person's "hot button," and respond to any questions or concerns. The development director should hold such visits at least annually.

Former board members often feel distant from the organization that they care about so deeply. Annual personal visits can connect them to organizational advances and trends in the field, while also allowing them to identify and state their own passions and interests about the organization. Invite former board members to participate in organizational activities—including building the endowment—and to attend upcoming events.

Prospective Bequest Donors

The organization's repeated message to consider a bequest will usually produce self-identified bequest prospects. Respond immediately and make a personal visit. After establishing a rapport with prospective donors, let them know that any information they share with you will be held in confidence, unless they give permission to reveal it to others. Draw from the prospective donors what they want to accomplish through the charitable bequest. Keep detailed records of discussions. Provide sample bequest language stating the full legal name, address, and tax identification number of the organization for prospective donors to share with their attorneys. Be sure that the organization's attorney has approved the draft language in advance. Both during the process of closing the gift and after the bequest has been completed, invite the donor to participate in the life of the organization—as a volunteer in a specific project of interest, through attendance at appropriate programs and events, and as a committee member.

Develop a system for tracking prospective bequest donors and donors who have finalized their bequest provisions. A coding system should be in place to readily identify this important relationship with the donor to anyone with access to the donor's records.

Families of Deceased Donors

Spouses and other family members of deceased endowment donors often have strong attachments to the charitable interests of their loved ones. They may want to participate in the organization that was important to the deceased spouse or parent and often appreciate the continuation of communication and involvement. Let's face it: Donors probably left more money to their family members than they did to the organization. Cultivate and involve those heirs for their own endowment gifts in the future.

At the time of the donor's death, attend the memorial service if possible and send a letter of condolence. After an appropriate amount of time, at least four to six weeks, send another note, perhaps with a small gift such as a book or a bookmark. Send periodic reports on how the distributions from the endowment are being used, and invite the family members to visit the organization and meet the people being served. Include the remaining spouse in the legacy society, and invite him or her to special events and activities. Send annual reports to all family members.

Life-Income Donors

During the giving process, as described in Chapter 4, provide full disclosure to the donor and the donor's advisors and family members. When life-income payments are made to the donor, try to include a personal note to the donor—perhaps simply a "thanks again" or general organizational news. If a financial institution is administering these payments for the organization, the development officer can send a separate letter or note, timed to arrive at about the same time that the check is being sent by the financial institution. At least once a year, hand-deliver the check to those donors who do not use direct deposit. When the development directors call to ask for visits to deliver checks, they are rarely turned down.

Life-income donors have made investments in the organization, and they want to know about the status of their investments. Inform donors about the organization and its new programs as well as the value of the anticipated gift. Invite these donors to join the legacy society. Be sure that they are included in all appropriate activities and are on the mailing list.

Donor Services Cautions

Balancing Effort and Effectiveness

Developing strong relationships with qualified prospective donors is vital to endowment building. However, some development officers spend unreasonable time and effort on prospective donors who have neither the intention nor the ability to complete charitable gifts. Good fundraisers learn to balance their time and the organization's money with the likelihood of future gifts. Neither the donors' nor the organizations' interests are well served when gift negotiation processes extend beyond reasonable limits. Experience and mentors can help new development officers learn when the expectation of a gift is unrealistic.

Gift Commitment

The development officer's goal is to obtain a current gift or a firm commitment to a future gift to the organization's endowment—or some other program. Some prospective donors may informally promise gifts, but avoid committing themselves to completing the gift arrangements. Some techniques to overcome this hurdle include the following:

More Thoughts About Donor Services

- Let the donor know that you value the friendship that has developed and that you will be in contact, even if there is never another gift. You have raised the expectations of the donor, and it is important that those expectations be fulfilled.

- Meet the needs of donors and they will talk to friends. In the commercial world, if a business loses one customer, it really loses eight because people talk to friends and colleagues. Reine Shiffman, a consultant with Reine A. Shiffman and Associates, Ltd., in Mendota Heights, Minnesota, says that only 4% of unhappy donors bother to complain. That means that for every complaint the development officer hears, 24 others were not heard.

- High-quality donor services encourage additional gifts not only from donors, but also from the donors' family members and friends. How donors are treated today will impact how their peers and family members will give in the future.

- Whatever the donor services techniques that are selected by the organization, it must remember that each donor is an individual, with different motives, interests, capabilities, and quirks. The donor services process should be tailored to fit the individual donor. They are friends, and they deserve to be treated as such.

- Ask a current donor to discuss the difficulty and benefits of committing a gift.

- Use a project or program time frame to encourage the gift completion. For example, "We are wrapping up the endowment portion of the capital campaign, and we want to be sure that your gift will be included. Can the gift we discussed be finalized in the next two weeks?"

- Ask the CEO or board chair to communicate the importance of finalizing the gift.

Donor Control

In the past, organizations identified prospective donors from their lists of constituents and asked for their financial support. Today, donors identify the charitable organizations with which they want to affiliate and expect the organizations to invest resources into building meaningful relationships. Many prospective donors are increasingly interested in controlling the gift-giving process and personally negotiating gifts. Others want to participate in decisions regarding the use of gifts after they have been given. These new expectations of donors challenge some forms of donor services and increase the skills needed to be effective development officers. Balancing the donor's desire to remain actively involved with the organization's established priorities and policies is an art that development officers acquire with experience.

Where Do We Go from Here?

Caring for donors and prospective donors is a critically important function of endowment building efforts, and it cannot be left to chance or instinct. Donor services must be carefully planned, while preserving a personal touch that must be customized for each person and family. The stewardship of donors and their advisors begins with the first contact and continues after the gift is completed—even after the donor's death.

The next chapter tackles the topic of marketing the endowment program to the organization's various constituencies and to the broad community. This is no small task. Taken one step at a time, endowment marketing can fold into the marketing strategies that the organization already has in place and offer additional marketing opportunities of its own.

Notes

1. Daniel Conway. "Practicing Stewardship." *Hank Rosso's Achieving Excellence in Fund Raising*, 2nd Edition, Eugene R. Tempel, editor. San Francisco, CA: Jossey-Bass, 2003, p. 433.

2. Betsy A. Mangone, "Spectacular Stewardship." 12th National Conference on Planned Giving, 1999.

3. Barbara L. Ciconte and Jeanne G. Jacob. *Fundraising Basics: A Complete Guide*, 2nd Edition, Gaithersburg, MD: Aspen Publishers, 2001.

CHAPTER 7

Marketing the Endowment

 After reading this chapter, you will be able to

- Define goals for the marketing program.
- Write an effective case statement for the endowment.
- Select criteria by which to choose marketing strategies.
- Segment prospective endowment donors.
- Develop core messages and themes to build awareness and understanding of the endowment.
- Develop tactics and tools to deliver the core messages to the appropriate markets.

If you always do what you always did, you will always get what you always got.

—Jackie "Moms" Mabley

"**D**on't be fooled," says Reine Shiffman, a planned giving consultant in the Minneapolis area. "Marketing is not just brochures. Or a quarterly newsletter. Marketing is the tenor of your organization. It's about the way in which your organization is projected. It's about the relationship you have with your donors. It is the way you are perceived from a communication and service orientation."[1]

The purpose of endowment marketing is to give prospective donors reasons to take action, cause a transaction to occur, get people to complete gifts or gift plans. Thus, marketing can be seen as the continuum from broad-based promotional strategies to one-on-one relationships resulting in current gifts and completed planned gifts.

Michael Kateman,[2] director of arts development and planning at the University of Missouri–Columbia, says that the three most important elements of a winning marketing strategy for planned giving are consistent promotion, personal contact, and positioning the organization's mission. The same applies to marketing endowments. Note that the first and third elements are often considered marketing tasks, whereas the second is usually assigned to the development office. In reality, the three elements must function seamlessly, as part of an organization-wide endowment building effort.

Some of the topics related to marketing have been covered in prior chapters. For example, Chapter 4 discussed the cultivation and personal solicitation of donors, and Chapter 6 described a variety of ways to develop deeper personal relationships with donors. This chapter defines the goals for the marketing program and incorporates marketing efforts into the Endowment Action Program, describes the framework for an effective case statement, lists criteria by which to select marketing strategies, discusses market segmentation of prospective endowment donors, and examines messages, tactics, and tools that are effective for building endowments.

Goals and the Written Marketing Program

The endowment marketing effort may be focused on one or two goals or may seek to accomplish several goals. The staff and board members should reach a consensus about the goals at the outset. Some of the goals might include the following:

- To give visibility to the organization and the people it serves.

- To increase public awareness of the endowment and its purposes.

- To create the expectation that donors will make bequests and other planned gifts eventually.

- To disseminate information about charitable gift provisions in wills and estate plans.

- To generate donor inquiries for endowment and planned giving information and services. Spur the donor to say, "Sounds interesting. Tell me more."

- To involve donors and prospects through their participation in testimonials or other marketing activities.

- To identify prospective donors—for the endowment and current programs.

- To educate prospective donors about the various ways to make endowment gifts and the implications of each.

- To motivate prospective donors to take action.

- To provide helpful information to professional advisors and increase their knowledge of the organization's endowment program.

- To recognize and thank the organization's endowment donors and their advisors.

- To encourage repeat gifts to endowment.

Involve staff, board members, and volunteers in selecting realistic marketing goals and designing the written marketing plan that will be folded into the Endowment Action Program. The Endowment Action Program, then, will become part of the organization's strategic plan. It is important to institutionalize the endowment by making sure that all appropriate functions and departments incorporate the endowment into their work plans—from the receptionist to the CEO and chair of the board.

The marketing portion of the Endowment Action Program is developed by selecting marketing strategies and tactics that can be tailored to specific groups of constituents for each organization. There is no cookie-cutter marketing plan that will work for all organizations; each must be customized to the specific circumstances of each organization's endowment. It is, however, universally true that a written marketing plan, even a very simple one, helps staff and volunteers keep their marketing efforts focused and effective. See Chapter 3 for more information about the Endowment Action Plan.

The Case Statement

The development of the marketing plan begins by designing a clear and compelling case statement. The case statement is based on the case for support, as discussed in Chapter 3.

The case statement reminds prospective donors what the organization does, who it serves, and why. It presents the organization's mission, vision, and goals as persuasively as possible so that a person will understand the benefits and importance of investing in the organization's future through an endowment gift. It outlines the organization's plans for programs and services and shows how this organization differs from similar organizations. It forms the foundation for future marketing, promotion, cultivation, and solicitation efforts, ensuring that all communication vehicles contain a consistent message and minimizing the effort that must be expended in writing future materials.

TIPS & TECHNIQUES

The Case Statement

The case statement answers questions that prospective donors are likely to ask, such as the following:

- What are the organization's mission and its vision of the future?

- How is it different from other organizations?

- Who is associated with the organization?

- Whom does the organization serve?

- How will economic or demographic trends affect those who are served?

- What problems and opportunities exist or are predicted to exist in the future?

- How does the organization address these issues, and how will it address them in the future?

- What is the role of the endowment in addressing these issues?

- Why should donors care?

- How does the endowment work?

- How will the donor's gift ensure that those who are served will benefit?

- How do donors feel about their gifts to the endowment?

- What are some of the specific giving opportunities, and what are their costs (e.g., campership endowment: $25,000; lecture series endowment: $100,000)?

- What is the commitment of the board to building the endowment, and how many members have made their own planned gift?

The case statement is usually drafted by one or more members of the development or marketing staff and then approved by the executive director and board.

Markets for Endowment Giving

The markets for endowment gifts must be identified, studied, and narrowed to create strategies that appeal to selected groups of people. This is particularly important for small and midsized organizations with limited marketing resources.

Individuals and Families

More than 90% of endowment gifts are from people—either through lifetime gifts or through their estates. Chapter 4 described the process of identifying prospective endowment donors. Some of the most important criteria include the following:

- Close ties to the organization through voluntarism and participation
- Evidence of shared values
- Service on the board of trustees
- Long history of giving to the organization
- Age 50 or older
- No close heirs
- History of endowment gifts to other organizations

People who fit one or more of these categories should be identified and screened to develop a list of prospects prioritized for endowment gifts. See the Considerations for Selecting Marketing Strategies section later in this chapter for criteria to prioritize prospective endowment donors.

Foundations and Corporations

Foundations and corporations rarely make gifts to endowments, but some will contribute to building the organizational capacity to begin or restart an endowment building program. They may be willing to fund marketing materials, Web site upgrades, staffing, or technology to track endowment donors and planned gifts. Some corporations and foundations contribute challenge or matching gifts that provide incentives for individuals to give, with the understanding that such gifts will be matched or multiplied in some way.

Keep the appropriate people informed about the progress of the endowment at corporations and foundations that make annual gifts to the organization. Although businesses often prefer to make direct gifts to current programs rather than endowments, the owners of businesses with long-term relationships with the organization may be personally interested in supporting the endowment. Be sure that these constituents receive mailings and materials about the endowment and invitations to seminars or workshops.

Allied Professionals

The professional advisors that prospective donors rely on are critically important allies in the gift planning process. They can make or break a gift arrangement. Strategies to engage them and build trusting relationships with them were discussed in Chapter 6. Marketing strategies must be employed to inform professional advisors about the organization's mission and endowment program, clarify the exact legal name of the organization, provide them with information and materials to pass on to their clients who are interested in the organization, and encourage their own personal involvement and financial support.

Inform the local professional community about strategies before you market them to prospective donors. The development officer should make it easy for professional advisors to work with the organization.

Ask donors for the names of their professional advisors. Identify and research the local attorneys who practice estate and tax planning as well as the local tax accountants. Identify constituents who are accountants, attorneys, bankers, stock brokers, and financial advisors. Add the contact information of all advisors who are connected to the organization in any way to a professional advisors mailing list. They need to receive regular communication from the organization.

Be prepared to respond to inquiries from professional advisors and other interested community members by creating resource packets about the organization, both electronically and in print. The packet should contain organizational and program information, material about the endowment, legal and tax identification information, and information about making charitable bequests to the organization. Offer luncheon programs and continuing education seminars for professional advisors.

In-house Team

Because the work of building the endowment reaches far beyond the development office, the development director must develop strategies to educate colleagues about the endowment and to enlist their help in cultivating and involving prospective endowment donors. The key "family" partners include members of the board of directors, the CEO, other development officers, the treasurer and members of the business office, and senior staff members. Each of these people should understand:

- How the endowment will provide for the long-term health of the entire organization
- How their efforts relate to the growth of the endowment
- How the endowment works
- How prospective donors to the endowment will be identified, cultivated, and asked for gifts

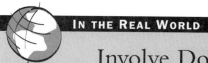

In the Real World

Involve Donors in Marketing

If involvement leads to commitment, then the marketing process is a perfect opportunity to involve prospects and donors. When endowment donors are profiled in the newsletter or annual report, they get lots of positive feedback from their peers, which increases their personal satisfaction with the gift they have made and the organization to which it was made. I once videotaped a prospective donor for an organization's campaign video. She had an opportunity to express her greatest hopes for that organization and the community, and to do so on videotape. She ultimately arranged a $500,000 planned gift to the organization.

—Laura MacDonald, Benefactors Counsel in Columbus

Strategies to share this information include informal get-togethers, small luncheons, breakfast discussions, quizzes over the local e-mail network, organized meetings, specialized communications, and seminars.

Marketing Strategies and Tools

Marketing plans define what will be done, how, where, when, and by whom. The likelihood of meeting goals and exceeding expectations increases with thorough planning—and then executing the plan. Make marketing strategies measurable so that the organization will know which strategies produced the best results for planning in the future.

Prospect Self-Identification

The endowment marketing program encourages prospective donors to self-identify themselves, to let the organization know that they are interested. Some of the ways to provide opportunities for self-identification are as follows:

- Include response mechanisms with all mailings to allow prospective donors to request endowment information. Add this to all membership renewals, annual fund solicitations, quarterly newsletters, and so forth.

- Create a special endowment mailing with a response mechanism for further information, a visit, or notice to the organization that a gift has already been completed.

- Develop Web site interactivity to encourage donors to request further information—or even to inform the organization of established gifts.

- Provide the name and contact information of the appropriate person to call for further information in all communications and articles.

- Tuck endowment flyers—with response cards—into envelopes with acknowledgment letters for current donors.

Direct Mail

Direct mail can reach the largest number of people for the least amount of cost. The challenge is to send a compelling message in an effective format to people who are interested, which is no small task. Even with this broad-based medium, it is important that the signatory of the letter be a peer of the recipient rather than the development officer or executive director. An enclosed newsletter, flyer or brochure can provide additional relevant information.

Consider using a one-line statement on all materials and stationery to encourage endowment gifts. For example, "Have you considered a gift to (the organization's) endowment through your will or estate plan?" Harvey DeVries, former vice president of public affairs for Bethel College and Seminary, suggests this tag line: "Every friend of Our Charity, Inc. should have a will, and every will should have a provision for Our Charity, Inc."

Design Materials with Prospective Donors in Mind

Effective endowment materials have several characteristics in common. Such materials:

- *Establish an emotional link between the organization and the prospective donor.* Donors give endowment gifts to the organizations that are the most important to them and with which they have the strongest bonds.

- *Are brief and to the point.* Give important data in small bites that are easy to understand. The goal is to provide enough information that the reader will take the initiative to respond, not to explain every detail and nuance in the newsletter or fact sheet.

- *Are easy to read.* Many of your prospective donors now need bifocals, so give them a break. The size and style of the type font and the color contrast are critically important elements for older eyes. Provide "white space" so the eyes can rest.

- *Use visuals that showcase the organization's good work.* People look at the graphics and pictures first. Make sure that the headlines, captions, and sidebars communicate your essential message, because some readers will read no further.

- *Use bulleted lists and pull quotes to emphasize important points.* These elements help break up dense blocks of text and are key points of focus for readers.

- *Include a postscript.* Readers may skip the body of the letter, but they nearly always read the P.S. Make sure it includes a call to action.

CONTINUED

TIPS & TECHNIQUES (CONTINUED)

- *Are professional and attractive but do not appear to be overly expensive.* The organization's competitors set the local standard. What are donors receiving from other organizations? Most donors want the distributions from their endowment gifts to serve the mission, not make flashy brochures.

- *Are consistent with the look and feel of the organization's other publications.* The continuity of the organization's image and message reduces confusion for its donors.

Newsletters

Newsletters, whether in print or electronic format, are usually sent to the broadest audience. Remember that the primary goals for endowment marketing strategies are to inform people about the endowment building program and to generate inquiries from motivated prospects. Be sure to include a response card or contact information with endowment articles in each issue. Repetition is good, because most donors need to hear or read the same message several times before acting to learn more about endowment gifts.

Endowment Mailing

Send out an endowment mailing that includes, at a minimum, a fact sheet or brochure and a personalized cover letter. The mailing explains the ways in which a planned gift to the endowment can make a difference and solve a problem for the donor. It is most effective when sent to defined subgroups of the constituency to reach prospective donors in specific circumstances. For example, the mailing might describe charitable gift annuities for those near retirement age.

Message Testing

Before going public with new materials or new messages, test them on constituents. Hold a candid discussion, promising that no comments will be attributed to specific individuals. Invite a group of people to lunch, host a donor roundtable, meet one-on-one with selected individuals, conduct a survey, or hold a focus group with an outside facilitator. The format is not as important as the openness of the staff to honest feedback. Participation in these test sessions builds the participants' ownership and commitment to the endowment and encourages them to consider their own endowment gifts.

Special Events

Exhibit openings, open houses for organizational facilities, scholarship receptions, retirement parties, and other special events can be appropriate events to market endowments, especially endowment funds designated for specific purposes. As the event is being planned, determine if all or a portion of the proceeds will be added to the endowment. If so, publicize that fact and the benefits of the endowment to the organization's clients. Perhaps a special exhibit or table about the endowment at the event would be appropriate.

Seminars or Workshops

Seminars or workshops about planned giving and estate planning can be an effective way to provide education about seemingly complex issues and, at the same time, showcase the organization and its programs. In addition to sending invitations or flyers, with response envelopes, to appropriate members of the organization's constituencies, place articles in the newsletter with response cards, and include a phone number for inquiries. An advertisement in the local newspaper may be appropriate as well. Before the workshop, plan the follow-up with all participants—a letter, phone call, or visit. At the workshop, give each participant a form to request a no-obligation personal visit.

Web Site

Include well-designed and easy-to-navigate endowment building pages on the organization's Web site. These pages can provide information about the endowment, ways to contribute, form language for a bequest, interactive opportunities to calculate planned gifts, and links to other sites with useful information and articles. Provide contact information for appropriate staff members with a reply e-mail button on each Web page.

Group Presentations

Offer to make presentations about the endowment to affiliated organizations (such as alumni groups and volunteer associations) and social, fraternal, and civic groups. Many groups meet monthly and are looking for speakers about organizations that are vital to the community. Consider taking along a person

TIPS & TECHNIQUES

Other Marketing Tactics

Organizations use a wide variety of strategies to reach prospective and current endowment donors, such as the following:

- Statement stuffers to alumni, patients, annual givers, and so on

- Check-off boxes on annual membership forms or in reunion mailings

- Advertisements in the organization's publications and in the local print and electronic media

- Blast e-mail

- Stuffers in monthly statements from utility companies, banks, and others who may have benefited from the endowment fund to provide a first-person testimonial to its value.

Group Gatherings

Small-group gatherings based on a common affiliation such as neighborhoods, professions, interests, and social groups can be effective methods to motivate people to act and to tell others about the organization's services and its endowment. A steering committee should establish guidelines for the gatherings, including purpose, content, timing, responsibilities of hosts, follow-up, and evaluation. The staff should develop discussion toolkits, and the steering committee should select hosts from various backgrounds, geographic locations, professions, and age ranges. Hosts compile the guest lists and work with the staff to include current donors and new participants in the constituency group. Publicity about the gatherings will increase visibility for the organization.

Personal Phone Calls

Board members often contact prospects to arrange a meeting between the prospective donor and the organization's development officer. This personal contact is frequently the key to establishing the personal visit. See Chapter 4 for more about the initial contact.

Personal Visits

The best marketing strategy for endowment funds is the personal visit. All other cultivation and marketing strategies are aimed at obtaining an appointment to visit face-to-face with prospective donors. Notice that these encounters are called visits—not meetings, interviews, or solicitations. Personal visits develop personal relationships between the individuals involved, which lead to long-term trust and confidence in the organization. Chapter 4 discusses personal visits in detail.

Recognition

Appropriate and heartfelt recognition for endowment donors gives honor to their gifts and provides models for others to follow as they consider their own endowment gifts. Chapter 6 describes the gift recognition process and specific recognition strategies.

The annual report should list donors' names by categories or gift levels. Gift levels are considered important strategies to encourage donors to stretch to the next level. The listing provides recognition for major donors. According to Laura MacDonald, president of Benefactors Counsel in Columbus, some organizations are developing guidelines for donor and volunteer recognition that differentiate donors based on criteria other than gift size, focusing on desirable donor behaviors such as gifts for endowment, recurring gifts, increased gifts, and cumulative giving. Other strategies may recognize desirable actions from volunteers, such as recruiting new donors.

If possible, donors should be involved in designing and reviewing forms of public recognition. Do not assume that donors will enjoy a surprise. In acknowledgment letters sent to endowment donors, add a sentence such as: "Your gift makes you eligible for membership in the legacy society, and you will be listed as a member in the annual report, unless you request otherwise." Other forms of public recognition, such as feature articles, should be approved by the donor in advance. If the donor has asked for anonymity, that request is always honored.

Develop an article in the annual report about the endowment's growth and the uses of its distributions, and list endowment donors directly under the article. This tactic provides donor recognition and publicity for the endowment. Publicity about individual gifts is often reserved for the largest gifts, which perpetuates the belief that all endowment donors are wealthy and that gifts to endowment are always very large. Consider press releases about donors in interesting circumstances or with unique backgrounds whose gifts are more modest. Tell the stories of individuals and families who make endowment gifts, what motivated them to do so, and how the gift will make life better for real people—in the newspaper, if possible, and in the organization's newsletter.

Tracking Marketing Strategies

With all of these strategies to chose from, it is important to understand which strategy is intended to produce what outcome. Exhibit 7.1 may help everyone involved understand the expected outcomes.

Considerations for Selecting Marketing Strategies

Marketing strategies, as evidenced by the preceding discussion, are almost limitless. Paring down the options to those that will be most appropriate and effective is important to avoid scattered efforts that do not yield desired results.

EXHIBIT 7.1

Endowment Marketing Strategies Chart

	Make Case	Build Case	Generate Leads	Qualify Leads	Close Gifts	Donor Relations	Repeat Gifts
Direct mail	X	X	X				
Special events	X		X			X	
Advertising	X	X					
Web site	X	X	X			X	
Group gatherings	X	X	X				
Seminars	X	X	X				X
Newsletters	X	X	X			X	X
Personal visits	X	X	X	X	X	X	X
Recognition		X	X			X	X

The staff and volunteers involved in marketing the endowment must understand the individual donor's needs and wants and then tailor marketing efforts to the particular needs and interests of different audiences. Here are some criteria to consider during this selection process.

TIPS & TECHNIQUES

Strategies for Baby Boomers

Identify what particular audiences value and then consider what your organization can offer to those markets. For example, consider Baby Boomers—those born between 1945 and 1964. They frequently value:

- Simplicity and convenience

- Straight talk and good information about things that affect them

- Accountability

- Excellent quality and service

- Having concerns addressed promptly

- Making a difference in the world

Develop a marketing strategy around their values, bond them to the organization, give them increased accountability, and provide them with instant gratification. Determine the parts of the organization's mission that are likely to appeal to this market segment. Play up those features, telling stories about people the organization serves and about people who give to the organization, especially to the endowment.

Recognize that Boomers have financial concerns, such as college funding for children, future needs of aging parents, and adequate savings and investments for retirement. They may hold appreciated assets—both securities and real property—and may have contributed the limit to retirement plans. They are looking for ways to diversify portfolios without paying capital gains tax; for supplemental funding for retirement, children's

TIPS & TECHNIQUES (CONTINUED)

education, and/or aging parents; and for charitable income-tax deductions to offset high earning years.

Charitable organizations might appeal to Boomers by creating fact sheets about the following topics

- How a deferred charitable gift annuity can provide the donor with retirement income and also provide for the organization as the ultimate beneficiary

- How charitable remainder trusts or gift annuities can provide funding for college educations and also provide for the organization as the ultimate beneficiary

- How charitable gift annuities can provide income for parents and also provide for the organization as the ultimate beneficiary

- For property owners, how the use of a charitable remainder trust might be beneficial to them when they are ready to sell their property and also provide for the organization as the ultimate beneficiary

- Ways to create a named endowment with several small gifts paid over three to five years that can be invested for the organization's eventual use, say, when it reaches $50,000

[Adapted from Reine Shiffman's presentation, "Marketing Planned Gifts: Theory Meets Practical—An Encounter of the Successful Kind," at the National Conference on Planned Giving in 2000.]

Note that these are not ideas or materials that describe generic charitable gift annuities or remainder trusts. They talk about how a particular charitable gift plan can address a prospective donor's particular need. The marketing program encourages people to hear or read about the organization based on their needs. Also note that Reine describes fact sheets that can be updated and personalized quickly, rather than fancy preprinted brochures. The more simple and personalized the approach is, the more likely the recipient is to read and respond to it.

Wealth

Because giving to endowment is often through planned gifts, the ability to make a significant gift is measured by accumulated assets, rather than by current earnings. Some people may earn large annual salaries but spend everything they earn on lifestyle choices and obligations to others. They are usually not good prospective endowment donors. Those who have accumulated assets—whether in the form of cash, securities, real estate, tangible property, or retirement savings—are better able and more likely to consider investing in the organization's endowment.

However, do not limit marketing only to the wealthy in an endowment program. Individuals and families of modest means have strong desires to invest in the future of their communities. Many have saved and accumulated assets of surprising sizes, as *The Millionaire Next Door*[3] so vividly recounts. Some people purchase insurance policies for fractions of their face values. Others give through their wills, sometimes treating their favorite charities like another member of the family. Endowment marketing should include donors at all income and asset levels.

Age

Endowment building appeals primarily to mature donors who are in or past their prime earning years (50 plus)—those same people who comprise the largest wave of aging consumers in history. Thus, organizations that seek to engage endowment donors focus their marketing approaches to give more attention to older markets. In *Ageless Marketing*, David B. Wolfe says, "By 2010, spending by people 45 and older will be a trillion dollars greater than spending by people between the ages of 18 and 39—$2.6 trillion to $1.6 trillion."[4] These same people are more likely to have accumulated assets, in addition to current income, and fewer financial responsibilities and commitments, because their children are likely raised and educated and their homes owned mortgage-free.

As people age, they are more likely to think about their place in the cosmic scheme of things. The National Committee on Planned Giving's 2000 survey[5] found that planned gift donors, on average, made their first bequest at a mean age of 58. Thus, one-half of the bequest donors were less than 58, so do not completely discount younger prospective donors, especially in encouraging their involvement with the organization as volunteers and annual donors. Nonetheless, focus your endowment building marketing programs on people age 50 and older.

Given this focus, age-related changes in people age 50 and older are important considerations as organizations design their endowment marketing program. Virtually every sensory system, as well as the musculoskeletal system and brain function, are affected by the aging process. Two sensory systems are particularly important for development and marketing directors to consider:

1. *Sight.* By the time eyes are 50 years old, they have lost their ability to maintain a crisp, clear image regardless of the quality and angle of light. This is critically important in print and electronic communication vehicles, as David B. Wolfe describes:

   > Changes in visual acuity call for special consideration in choosing font style and font size, paper finish, color of paper, and inks. Reverse type (white type on a dark background), which is commonly used ostensibly to get attention, is especially problematic. A brochure or ad may win an award for creative excellence, but fail in its primary purpose if type size, ink choices, and glare thrown off by a high-gloss finish discourage a person from reading the brochure or ad.[6]

2. *Hearing.* By their early fifties, many people begin experiencing decreased sensitivity to frequencies at both ends of the sound spectrum. Loud restaurants and booming music turns off older people. Literally. Another issue is the slowing central nervous system, which can no longer process sounds and their meanings at the same fast pace of younger central nervous systems. Slow down explanations of technical material and make one point at a time.

Location of the Donor

Some nonprofits serve local constituencies, whereas others reach out regionally and nationally. The location of donors may drive the method used to reach those donors. Even when donors are dispersed across the United States, try to personalize marketing materials and keep in personal contact—if not in person, then by telephone.

Maturity of the Organization

Organizations that have been providing services for many years will usually have greater community recognition and track records, and thus be able to build a case for their longevity and the importance of an endowment for the future. A younger organization may need to devote more energy to making the case for its mission and long-term viability.

Availability of Volunteers

Organizations with large groups of engaged volunteers may be able to undertake labor-intensive visits and special events, whereas organizations without volunteers must look for ways to communicate with and attract support that do not involve as much personal time commitment. Volunteers, especially long-term volunteers, are often good prospective endowment donors as well.

Depth of the Staff

The goal of the marketing effort, as stated previously, is to generate inquiries for follow-up. Be sure that the staff is in place to handle the responses in a timely manner and that the staff is trained to do so. (See staffing and budget recommendations in Chapter 3.)

Compelling Themes and Messages

Marketing the endowment offers opportunities to emphasize several unique and compelling themes and messages to appropriate constituent groups through a variety of marketing strategies.

Naming Opportunities

Endowment gifts, above a certain minimum value established by the organization, can be named for the donor or the donor's family. They give the donor the opportunity to honor the life or memory of a colleague or loved one *in perpetuity*. Some organizations prepare written listings of naming opportunities and their corresponding costs to raise donors' philanthropic sights. Many named endowment funds begin with a minimum of $10,000, although some may start at $50,000 up to $500,000. For example, scholarship funds may start at $50,000 simply to produce a meaningful scholarship annually ($50,000 times 5% is $2,500 per year). Endowing a faculty chair would have a larger minimum ($1 million to $1.5 million). The bottom line is that the endowment needs to produce enough money to be meaningful, to make a difference.

Named Endowment Fund Agreement

One of the best tools for closing endowment gifts is a customized draft named endowment fund agreement. Starting with the board-approved generic language (see Tips & Techniques for a sample bare-bones named endowment fund agreement in Chapter 3), insert a short biographical sketch of the donor(s) and the fund's purpose and any restrictions on the use of the fund's distributions. Encourage the donor's participation in the drafting process to build commitment to the fund's establishment and understanding of the fund's administration.

Endow Annual Gifts

Loyal, steady donors understand that their annual support is important to the organization's ongoing operations and budget. By explaining that their $1,000 annual gift could become a source of support *forever* with an endowment of $20,000 ($20,000 times 5% equals $1,000), the organization can encourage its steady donors to consider planned gifts to take effect when they are no longer here to make their annual gifts.

Endowment Fields of Interest

Donors are often particularly interested in and devoted to one specific area in which the organization is involved—patient care, lecture series, research, exhibits, teaching, outreach—rather than the organization as a whole. By providing a menu of broad fields of interest, the organization can encourage endowment gifts directed to the areas of work that are organizational priorities.

Specific Endowment Projects

Endowments can be successfully used to promote specific projects in which the organization is confident that it will always need support—professorships, scholarships, staff enrichment, facility operations—in connection with certain special events or anniversary celebrations. Universities have made good use of this concept with class endowment funds, especially for 50th reunion classes. The retirement of revered staff members or CEOs can successfully promote an endowment in the honoree's name. A capital campaign for a new or expanded facility often includes an endowment component to provide for the building's future upkeep.

Memorial Gifts

Memorial gifts for endowment are a natural fit, because loved ones, friends, and colleagues often seek meaningful ways to express their appreciation for the life of someone special. The permanence of the endowment is particularly appealing, as well as the ongoing support that will be produced for the important work of the organization, both now and forever.

Legacy Society

The legacy society or other recognition group established to honor those who have made planned gifts can be particularly useful when promoted effectively and administered professionally. Most people enjoy recognition, appreciate occasional opportunities to socialize with peers, and look forward to insider treatment with organizations that are important to them. It can also offer a softer way to approach donors: "I hope you'll join me as a member of the Legacy Society's Endowment Investors Club" rather than "I hope you'll make a $20,000 gift to the endowment." See more about this topic in Chapter 6.

Stewardship Benefits

The stewardship and recognition benefits discussed in Chapter 6 are appealing to some donors. Publicize such benefits as the wall of honor and the listing in the annual report for the endowment donors and the permanent nature of named endowments.

Stories of Real People

Personal donor stories should be included in every issue of the newsletter and told to prospects at every opportunity—with the donor's permission. The stories of real gifts from real people inspire others to give and affirm the gifts of donors who have made lasting investments in the organization.

Where Do We Go from Here?

The endowment offers a plethora of marketing opportunities and ways to connect donors more closely to the organization. Many of the strategies described in this chapter may already be in use by the organization for other fundraising programs. A new endowment building effort often means strategically adding to existing marketing programs and adding a few new tools specifically targeted to prospective endowment donors and their advisors.

The last chapter of this book describes methods to measure success and evaluate endowment building strategies. As the next chapter makes clear, measurements of success are more than financial alone.

Notes

1. Reine Shiffman. "Marketing Planned Gifts: Theory Meets Practical—An Encounter of the Successful Kind." 13th National Conference on Planned Giving, 2000.

2. Michael Kateman, "Planning to Market and Marketing the Plan: An Overview of Marketing Planned Gifts," National Conference on Planned Giving, 1999.

3. Thomas J. Stanley and William D. Danko. *The Millionaire Next Door.* Atlanta, GA: Longstreet Press, 1996.

4. David B. Wolfe with Robert E. Snyder. *Ageless Marketing.* Chicago, IL: Dearborn Trade Publishing, 2003, p. 23.

5. "Planned Giving in the United States 2000: A Survey of Donors." National Committee on Planned Giving, 2001.

6. Wolfe with Snyder, p. 306.

CHAPTER 8

Measuring Success

After reading this chapter, you will be able to

- Define success for the endowment building efforts—both short- and long-term.

- Measure the cost and benefit of the Endowment Action Program.

- Base measurements on goals, external standards, and strategies described in the Endowment Action Plan.

- Develop collaborative assistance from all departments and functions of the organization.

- Select and refine performance indicators.

- Develop spreadsheets to measure results and to project future gifts and investment returns.

How different our lives are when we really know what is deeply important to us, and keeping that picture in mind, we manage ourselves each day to be and to do what really matters most.

—Stephen Covey

T he success of endowment building efforts is measured by donor satisfaction, standards of performance of staff and board members, the number and amount of gifts to principal, total return on investments, and gift expectancies (gifts that have been executed but not yet received). These measurements and others are based on goals, external standards, and strategies described in the Endowment Action Plan, with financial, marketing, and development components. At the same time, don't focus so much on these numbers that you lose sight of what's really important: the impact of the endowment on those you serve.

Endowment building is always a group effort, and many people and departments have a hand in the success of endowment building efforts for charitable organizations. The leadership of the board of directors and its members is critically important in terms of hands-on involvement and accountability, personal financial commitment, securing the necessary organizational resources to conduct an effective program, and public support of the organization. The executive director's enthusiastic involvement in helping to develop the Endowment Action Program, providing personal and moral support to the staff, integrating the endowment building efforts into the organization's comprehensive strategic plan, and meeting with prospective donors is imperative. Through collaborative efforts, the staff in the business, marketing, and development departments implement the strategies and tactics enumerated in the Endowment Action Program and enable donors to articulate and realize their charitable dreams. All of these people directly affect the success of the endowment building program.

This chapter discusses ways to define the success of endowment building and how to measure the cost and benefit of the Endowment Action Program and its related strategies and tactics. Because endowment building is a long-term effort, it can be difficult to determine the benefits of the program in the short run. Yet such a determination is necessary to evaluate the performance of individuals, departments, and the organization; to plan for future endowment growth; and to justify the organization's investment of resources in the program.

Performace Indicators

Because endowment building is a long-term process often without immediate results, performance indicators in addition to gifts and expectancies are important to measure. This is particularly true in the first few years of an endowment building program when gifts and assets will be limited. The performance indicators should directly relate to the Endowment Action Program's strategies and the goals for each activity.

Marketing goals, for example, could be measured in terms of generating opportunities for follow-up with donors. A direct mail goal might be as simple as the generation of a 1% or 2% response rate yielding five inquiries. Reasonable seminar goals could be to attract 20 participants from 200 to 300 invitees, and to generate two follow-ups. A newsletter article about bequests to the endowment might be sent to 4,000 people, inspire 20 responses, and secure three new legacy society members through follow-up calls. These goals would be compared with the actual results.

Here are some activities to measure against the goals established in the Endowment Action Plan:

- Phone calls by development officers or volunteers to donors or prospects
  - Number made
  - Number responding to inquiry
  - Number and percentage that resulted in personal visits
- Personal visits by development officers or volunteers to donors or prospects
  - Number held
  - Number of prospects moved closer to completing a gift
  - Number of visits that resulted in gifts
  - Number of follow-up visits after the gift receipt/commitment was made

- Personal letters or notes to donors or prospects
  - Number sent
  - Number responding to inquiry
  - Number that included an enclosure
  - Number and percentage that resulted in personal visits
- Direct mail
  - Number of mailings and number of pieces sent
  - Inquiry response rate from each mailing
  - Gift rate from each mailing
  - Number that resulted in personal visits
- Web site
  - Number of hits to the endowment section
  - Length of stay in the endowment/planned giving section
  - Number of queries made through Contact Us
- Publicity
  - Number of articles about the endowment in the organization's newsletter
  - Number and length of articles in print and electronic media
- Events
  - List each event and its purpose
  - Number attending each event
  - Number of inquiries following each event
- Legacy Society
  - Number of new members
  - Number of total members
  - Number of repeat donors

- Professional Advisors
  - ○ Number of phone calls with professional advisors
  - ○ Number of personal meetings with advisors
  - ○ Number of referrals from advisors

In order to track these activities, sources of inquiries, activities, and results must be recorded on a spreadsheet. Although not all activities and results can be tracked or measured—such as that important marketing tool, word of mouth—it is well worth the effort to document as much as possible for annual evaluation purposes and for annual reports to the board.

Endowment Gifts

Gifts to the endowment are the easiest measurement of the endowment building program. Keep in mind that most gifts are the result of many variables—such as the organization's history and excellent reputation, innovative new projects and services developed over the past several years, and the work of many board and staff members in cultivating and engaging donors during an extended period.

When calculating endowment gifts, list only gifts that were actually received by the nonprofit organization during the fiscal year. Use a cash basis rather than an accrual basis to count gifts. This report can include all planned gifts or only gifts for the endowment, according to the needs of the organization. Annually prepare a report that lists the following:

- Planned giving (or endowment gifts or both) in total
- Planned giving (or endowment gifts or both) by gift type (number of gifts and dollar amount):
  - ○ Cash
  - ○ Publicly traded securities
  - ○ Closely held securities

- o Real estate
- o Tangible property
- o Charitable lead trusts
- Number and value of gifts received in response to specific marketing tactics
- Number and value of gifts received in response to specific development tactics

If the report includes all planned gifts, track gifts designated for the endowment separately. After the first year, prepare a report comparing the current year's gifts with the gifts received in the prior year or years. Consider using a chart to make the comparison. The numbers in any given year may be low or high, but over time a growth pattern should emerge. In time, these reports should paint a positive picture of the growth of the endowment and the growth of gifts annually.

Endowment Investment Results

Investment results are another important measurement of the success of the endowment building program. The endowment's investment results should be measured against appropriate benchmarks—such as the Dow Jones or Standard & Poor's average—identified in the investment and spending policies rather than against some predetermined monetary or percentage goal. As the endowment grows over the years, the investment managers should prepare cumulative charts showing its growth over the past three, five, and ten years compared to the benchmarks. These calculations can be tricky and should be carefully monitored to be sure that they are accurate and compare "apples to apples." See the Steven L. Mourning article referenced in Chapter 5, and work with the business office and the organization's financial and investment advisors to develop a standard reporting format and process.

Endowment Projections

It is helpful to demonstrate to the staff and the board how the endowment is projected to grow in the next few years, especially when the endowment building program is in its infancy and there are no or very few gifts or assets to report. Such a report will also provide benchmarks against which the program can measure its growth in the future.

Exhibit 8.1 is a basic six-line spreadsheet titled Endowment Projections. Begin with the present value of the endowment at the beginning of the year. On the next line, plug in a realistic total return on the present value, measured as a percentage (perhaps 6% to 10%) of the endowment value at the beginning of the year. On the third line, add the amount the board has budgeted to the endowment from unrestricted gifts or from the organization's surplus. Add gifts designated for endowment projected to be received during the year as the fourth line. On the fifth line, subtract the net assets released (perhaps 4% to 5% of the rolling average of three to five years' beginning values). The total of these five figures is the projected endowment value at the end of the year. Use the current year's end-of-year value as the first line of a projection for next year, and so forth.

The spreadsheet might look something like this:

EXHIBIT 8.1

Endowment Projections

	Year 1	Year 2	Year 3	Year 4	Year 5
Endowment value, start of year					
Endowment growth (endowment value, start of year x 8%)					
Board designated contributions					
Gifts expected during year					
Less net assets released (3-year average value, start of year x 5%)					
Endowment value, end of year					

EXHIBIT 8.2

Endowment Projections Compared with Actual Results

	Year 1 Projected	Year 1 Actual
Endowment value, start of year		
Endowment growth (endowment value, start of year x 8%)		
Board designated contributions		
Gifts received during year		
Less net assets released (3-year average value, start of year x 5%)		
Endowment value, end of year		

Exhibit 8.2 is a sample spreadsheet to compare endowment projections to actual results at the end of the year.

At the end of each year, change projections for the future year to reflect the actual results.

Expectancies Confirmed

Executed charitable gift plans that will benefit the organization in the future are known as *expectancies*. Expectancies include bequests, charitable gift annuities, charitable remainder trusts, life insurance policies, and life estates. It is challenging and important to track the number and current value of expectancies in order to measure endowment building success. A new tool has recently been developed by the National Committee on Planned Giving to assist business offices in determining the value of expectancies, and it can be downloaded at *www.ncpg.org* for free. (See Tips & Techniques.)

TIPS & TECHNIQUES

Valuation Standards
for Charitable Planned Gifts

The National Committee on Planned Giving (NCPG) published *Valuation Standards for Charitable Planned Gifts* in 2004. Developed by an NCPG task force over a three-year period, the standards are designed to help charities determine the value of their planned gifts in terms of purchasing power.

The task force recognized that several methods for valuing planned gifts already existed, including the IRS charitable deduction and the Council for Advancement and Support of Education (CASE) gift crediting guidelines. It concluded, however, that none of the existing valuation methods adequately addressed the true worth of a planned gift to the nonprofit organization. The new standards are meant to provide the true worth of a planned gift to the organization by estimating the purchasing power of each planned gift in today's dollars.

Valuation data can be used by charitable organizations to:

- Evaluate the costs and benefits of planned gift fundraising.

- Determine the financial effectiveness of an organization's current investment in gift planning.

- Allocate appropriate resources to a gift planning program.

- Set planned gift fundraising expectations within a comprehensive fundraising program or campaign.

- Assess the effect of variables (e.g., term of the gift, investment strategy) on the ultimate value of the gift to the organization.

For purposes of valuation, expectancies can be divided into irrevocable commitments (unable to be changed, unalterable) and revocable commitments (able to be modified, rescinded or annulled). Methods for valuing each type of gift listed as follows are explained in the *Valuation Standards for Charitable Planned Gifts*. On an annual basis, the development officer should develop a chart that lists both the number and the present value of planned gifts in the following categories:

- Irrevocable commitments
  - Charitable gift annuity
  - Pooled income gifts
- Revocable commitments
  - Gift by will, specified amount
  - Gift by will, residual
  - Gift by trust, specified amount
  - Gift by trust, residual
  - Real estate
  - Tangible personal property
  - Charitable remainder unitrust (some may be irrevocable)
  - Charitable remainder annuity trust (some may be irrevocable)
  - Charitable gift annuity, testamentary
  - Charitable remainder unitrust, testamentary
  - Charitable remainder annuity trust, testamentary
  - Gifts with no estimated value
  - *Inter vivos* gifts

Although this list may seem complicated, realize that bequests through wills and trusts account for more than 85% of testamentary gifts to endowments for most institutions. The other kinds of gifts will be realized with less frequency, but it is important for the staff to understand how they "count" when reporting to the board.

EXHIBIT 8.3

Expectancy Projections

	Year 1	Year 2	Year 3	Year 4	Year 5
Expectancies, start of year					
New expectancies confirmed					
(Less expectancies realized or lost)					
Expectancies, end of year					

By sharing such reports with donors, the development officer will have an opportunity to bolster the donor's confidence in the organization's careful management of the endowment. Donors who are reluctant to reveal their personal charitable gift plans may be more likely to do so when they realize the importance of the information to the organization, as it plans for its future.

For purposes of reporting to the board of directors, prepare an Expectancy Projections spreadsheet (see Exhibit 8.3), similar to the Endowment Projections in Exhibits 8.1 and 8.2.

At the end of the year, prepare a report that compares the Expectancy Projections with the actual results (see Exhibit 8.4). Change future projections using actual results from the current year to begin the projections for the following year.

EXHIBIT 8.4

Expectancy Projections Compared with Actual Results

	Year 1 Projected	Year 1 Actual
Expectancies, start of year		
New expectancies confirmed		
(Less expectancies realized or lost)		
Expectancies, end of year		

EXHIBIT 8.5					
Endowment and Expectancy Projections					
	Year 1	Year 2	Year 3	Year 4	Year 5
Endowment value, end of year					
Expectancies, end of year					
Total endowment and expectancies					

Projections are only estimates, and the organization should not count on projections for budgeting purposes in any given year. Organizations that anticipate the receipt of planned gifts when they prepare budget projections are betting on the demise of their donors, a practice that is certainly distasteful and risks offending the members of the legacy society. Projections and expectancies are useful for planning purposes, not budget purposes, and tracking the effectiveness of planned giving strategies. Keep the program's champions enthusiastic.

Together, the endowment value at the end of the year and the expectancies at the end of the year give a clear indication of the progress of the endowment building program, especially when viewed over several years (see Exhibit 8.5).

Return on Investment

Because endowments are more than investments, the return on the investment may be best described as a social dividend in the future; the "good" that the endowment will achieve. Nonetheless, board members will want to know what has been accomplished as a result of the expenditure of resources to support the endowment program.

The return on investment for an endowment building program should be measured over several years—perhaps even a decade. Mature planned giving and endowment building programs often find that their total expenditures are 5% to 8% of the gifts received annually and less than 1% of the value of the endowment.

New endowment programs are different. Many endowment building programs combine their expenses with those of the total development effort, because the development department's expenses are more than offset by current operating gifts. Nonetheless, the author recommends that you measure the cost-benefit ratio of the endowment building program alone.

In Chapter 3, the staffing and budgeting needs of the endowment building program were discussed. Develop a chart to project the expenses the organization is likely to incur over the next few years. Exhibit 8.6 is an example of a spreadsheet to track the costs of a comprehensive endowment building program.

Some of these expenses will occur only one time or be higher in certain years than in others. For example, initially designing the planned giving/endowment building portions of the Web site will have higher costs than maintaining them in subsequent years.

Prepare a spreadsheet that demonstrates the relationship between the direct expenses of the endowment building program and the indicators of success described earlier in this chapter (see Exhibit 8.7).

The measurements of success enumerated in this chapter are indicators of the degree to which staff members and volunteers are consistently working the Endowment Action Program; donors are engaged in the long-term future of the organization and its work; the board has dedicated organizational resources to the endowment's growth; board members are leading the endowment building effort with their personal commitment of time and money; investment managers are appropriately investing the assets; and—most important—people will continue to be served by the organization, both now and in the future.

Going Forward

Endowment donors invest in the future. They seek organizations as partners to help them realize their visions for a better community or world.

EXHIBIT 8.6

Estimated Expenses

	Year 1	Year 2	Year 3	Year 4	Year 5
Personnel with benefits					
Development officer 1 (50–100% FTE)					
Development officer 2 (50–100% FTE)					
Finance officer (10% FTE)					
Marketing officer (10% FTE)					
President (10% FTE)					
Administrator (50–100% FTE)					
Staff training					
Print materials and postage					
Online materials and updating					
Web site enhancement and revisions					
Donor software/training/ maintenance					
Donor recognition					
Special events					
Workshop/seminar					
Legacy society reception					
Other events					
Travel					
Office supplies					
Consulting and outside services					
Legal and accounting					
Total Endowment Expenses					

EXHIBIT 8.7

Projections of Return on Investment

	Year 1	Year 2	Year 3	Year 4	Year 5
1. Gifts received					
2. Endowment value, end of year					
3. Total endowment and expectancies, end of year					
4. Direct expenses of endowment program					
Cost per dollar raised (4 divided by 1)					
Cost per dollar of endowment value (4 / 2)					
Cost per dollar of endowment and expectancies (4 / 3)					

The primary elements of successful endowment building programs can be summarized in six broad categories:

1. *Passion*. Those involved in building the endowment—board members, the CEO, development staff, marketing staff, finance staff, investment managers, and donors to the endowment—must be passionate about it. Without enthusiasm and vitality, the endowment effort will wither before endowment gifts are realized. The staff and volunteers must draw prospective donors closer to the organization and deepen the donors' loyalty to the organization.

2. *Planning and Preparation*. An Endowment Action Program—with goals, measurable objectives, and well-thought-out strategies—provides a framework for endowment activities and progress, and also provides a process to evaluate and refine tactics in the future. The executive director and board can use the plan to monitor progress and identify trouble spots that require additional resources or other intervention. Volunteers and staff members require training to be fully prepared to carry out the program

and to conduct one-on-one visits with prospective donors. Policies and procedures must be established, research completed, goals agreed upon, and strategies implemented.

3. *Performance Progression.* There must be a commitment to carrying out the Endowment Action Program, one step at a time. Development officers must get out of the office and meet people face-to-face. Marketing officers must send out the press releases and develop new materials. Finance professionals in the business office must track investments and performance benchmarks.

The work of endowment building involves small progressive steps taken over time: calling to establish a personal visit, gathering background information, developing relationships, telling stories, providing hands-on experiences, discussing values, presenting draft plans, working with professional advisors, closing gifts, recognizing donors, managing and investing assets, using distributions to help people, and publicizing positive results. Move each prospective donor along these progressive steps without bogging down at any one stage in the sequence.

4. *Persistence.* Go after it again and again. Regular and consistent communication with prospective donors is imperative. People need repeated messages and visits, time and again, year after year. If one strategy leads to a dead end, develop another strategy. Follow the Endowment Action Program, evaluate the results, adjust your tactics, and keep working.

Do not wait for donors to come to the organizations with their endowment gifts. Prospective donors usually have multiple responsibilities and many interests in their lives. Completing an endowment gift may be pushed aside in the rush of everyday activities. The development officer should help prospects and their advisors focus on charitable plans by making the giving process efficient and personally satisfying. The executive director should be the cheerleader, sustaining the enthusiasm of staff and volunteers alike during the early years.

5. *Partnering.* Endowment building is a group effort that includes donors, prospective donors, the organization as a whole, board members, volun-

teers, development professionals, other staff, professional advisors, donors' families, financial institutions, community foundations, and other allies. Keep all of the players involved and knowledgeable.

6. *Patience*. Donors act on their timeline, not the organization's time frame. Decisions about major charitable gifts require careful consideration, and some relationships require extra time to develop. Organizations must encourage prospective donors to take whatever time is necessary to be certain about and comfortable with their philanthropic commitments. Development officers work to carry out the Endowment Action Program, listen carefully to the prospective donor's comments and concerns, help resolve issues standing in the way of a gift, and respect the donor's time frame.

Endowment building is ongoing. It is also challenging and rewarding—both personally and professionally.

How lovely to think that no one need wait a moment; we can start now, start slowly changing the world.

—Anne Frank

Uniform Management of Institutional Funds Act (1972)

1. Definitions

In this Act

(a) "Institution" means an incorporated or unincorporated organization organized and operated exclusively for educational, religious, charitable, or other eleemosynary purposes, or a governmental organization to the extent that it hold funds exclusively for any of these purposes;

(b) "Institutional Fund" means a fund held by an institution for its exclusive use, benefit, or purposes, but does not include (i) a fund held for an institution by a trustee that is not an institution or (ii) a fund in which a beneficiary that is not an institution has an interest, other than possible rights that could arise upon violation or failure of the purposes of the fund;

(c) "Endowment fund" means an institutional fund, or any part thereof, not wholly expendable by the institution on a current basis under the terms of the applicable gift instrument;

(d) "Governing board" means the body responsible for the management of an institution or of an institutional fund;

(e) "Historic dollar value" means the aggregate fair value in dollars of (i) an endowment fund at the time it became an endowment fund, (ii) each subsequent donation to the fund at the time it is made, and (iii) each accumulation made pursuant to a direction in the applicable gift instrument at the time the accumulation is added to the fund. The determination of historic dollar value made in good faith by the institution is conclusive.

(f) "Gift instrument" means a will, deed, grant, conveyance, agreement, memorandum, writing, or other governing document (including the terms of any institutional solicitations from which an institutional fund resulted) under which property is transferred to or held by an institution as an institutional fund.

2. Appropriation of Appreciation

The governing board may appropriate for expenditure for the uses and purposes for which an endowment fund is established so much of the net appreciation, realized and unrealized, in the fair value of the assets of an endowment fund over the historic dollar value of the fund as is prudent under the standard established by Section 6. This Section does not limit the authority of the governing board to expend funds as permitted under other law, the terms of the applicable gift instrument, or the charter of the institution.

3. Rule of Construction

Section 2 does not apply if the applicable gift instrument indicates the donor's intention that net appreciation shall not be expended. A restriction upon the expenditure of net appreciation may not be implied from a designation of a gift as an endowment, or from a direction or authorization in the applicable gift instrument to use only "income," "interest," "dividends," or "rents, issues or profits," or "to preserve the principal intact," or a direction which contains other words of similar import. This rule of construction applies to gift instruments executed or in effect before or after the effective date of the Act.

4. Investment Authority

In addition to an investment otherwise authorized by law or by the applicable gift instrument, and without restriction to investments a fiduciary may make, the governing board, subject to any specific limitations set forth in the applicable gift instrument or in the applicable law other than law relating to investments by a fiduciary, may:

(a) Invest and reinvest an institutional fund in any real or personal property deemed advisable by the governing board, whether or not it produces a current return, including mortgages, stocks, bonds, debentures, and other securities of profit or not profit corporations, shares in or obligations of associations, partnerships, or individuals, and obligations of any government or subdivision or instrumentality thereof;

(b) Retain property contributed by a donor to an institutional fund for as long as the governing board deems advisable;

(c) Include all or any part of an institutional fund in any pooled or common fund maintained by the institution; and

(d) Invest all or any part of an institutional fund in any other pooled or common fund available for investment, including shares or interests in regulated investments companies, mutual funds, common trust funds, investment partnerships, real estate investment trusts, or similar organizations in which funds are commingled and investment determinations are made by persons other than the governing board.

5. Delegation of Investment Management

Except as otherwise provided by the applicable gift instrument or by applicable law relating to governmental institutions or funds, the governing board may (a) delegate to its committees, officer or employees of the institution or the fund, or agents, including investment counsel, the authority to act in place of the board in investments and reinvestment of institutional funds, (b) contract with independent investment advisors, investment counsel or managers, banks, or trust companies, so to act, and

(c) authorize the payment of compensation for investment advisory or management services.

6. Standard of Conduct

In the administration of the powers to appropriate appreciation, to make and retain investments, and to delegate investment management of institutional funds, members of a governing board shall exercise ordinary business care and prudence under the facts and circumstances prevailing at the time of the action or decision. In so doing they shall consider long- and short-term needs of the institution in carrying out its educational, religious, charitable, or other eleemosynary purposes, its present and anticipated financial requirements, expected total return on its investments, price level trends, and general economic conditions.

7. Release of Restriction on Use or Investment

(a) With the written consent of the donor, the governing board may release, in whole or in part, a restriction imposed by the applicable gift instrument on the use or investment of an institutional fund.

(b) If written consent of the donor cannot be obtained by reason of his death, disability, unavailability, or impossibility of identification, the governing board may apply in the name of the institution to the [appropriate] court for release of a restriction imposed by the applicable gift instrument on the use or investment of an institutional fund. The [Attorney General] shall be notified of the application and shall be given an opportunity to be heard. If the court finds that the restriction is obsolete, inappropriate, or impracticable, it may by order release the restriction in whole or in part. A release under this subsection may not change an endowment fund to a fund that is not an endowment fund.

(c) A release under this section may not allow a fund to be used for purposes other than the educational, religious, charitable, or other eleemosynary purposes of the institution affected.

(d) This section does not limit the application of the doctrine of cy pres.

8. Severability

If any provision of the Act or the application thereof to any person or circumstances is held invalid, the invalidity shall not affect other provisions or applications of the Act which can be given effect without the invalid provision or application, and to this end the provisions of this Act are declared severable.

9. Uniformity of Application and Construction

This Act shall be so applied and construed as to effectuate its general purpose to make uniform the law with respect to the subject of this Act among those states which enact it.

10. Short Title

This Act may be cited as the "Uniform Management of Institutional Funds Act."

Sample Questions for Prospective Donors

The questions that follow are designed to probe for information to develop and advance relationships, to increase engagement with the organization, and to lead to significant gifts for the endowment fund. Development officers and volunteers should select a few strategic questions from this list. Consider which questions are likely to yield the best information about the prospective donor's values.

(a) About the organization

- Why did you become involved with our organization?
- What did you hope to accomplish by your involvement?
- How do you feel about the organization and our work?
- What do you believe are the perceptions of our organization in the community, state, region, nationally?
- Which aspects of our programs do you believe are our greatest strengths?
- Do you have any particular concerns you would like me to share with our CEO, volunteer chair, board?

- What are your impressions of our CEO? Why?

- Have you had an opportunity to meet with any of the people we serve? Under what circumstances? What were your impressions?

(b) Mission, Vision, Endowment Program

- What are your impressions of our vision for the future?

- Do you believe we have a strong case for support of the endowment? If so, why? If not, why not?

- Among our fundraising priorities, which do you find the most compelling? Why? Least compelling? Why?

- If that (some objection to giving voiced before solicitation) was not an issue, in which of our priorities would you be interested?

- What other organizations do you perceive are our chief philanthropic competitors?

(c) Personal and Lifestyle (These questions are driven by prior knowledge or from observations at the home or office.)

- What are the ages and names of your children? Grandchildren? Where do they live? Do you get to see them often?

- Have you had a chance to take some time off this year? Is so, where did you go? If not, what would you like to do?

- How's business? How is this economy affecting you? Your business?

- How does the economy (your business situation) affect your philanthropic decisions?

- In what ways do your personal interests impact your volunteer activities and philanthropic investments?

(d) Philanthropy and Giving Interests

- What other organizations are you involved with? Volunteer for? On the board?

- Which are your top three? Why is that?

- Where is our organization on your list (if not among the top three)?
- What charitable gifts have given you the most satisfaction? Why?
- How did it come about? What made it so pleasurable? Are you still involved with them?
- Do you have any charitable provisions in your will? How did you decide to do that? Under what circumstances would you consider adding an additional provision or codicil?
- Have you ever made a gift using a planned giving vehicle like a trust or annuity? How did that come about?
- What factors go into your philanthropic decisions? How are decisions made at your house? Do you and (your spouse) make charitable decisions together?

(e) Involvement

- As you think about the most satisfying volunteer experience you've had, what was key?
- What one piece of advice would you give us as we plan our future?
- How can we get you more involved with our organization?
- We would love for you to (insert involvement request here). Is that something you would find of interest?

(f) Family Values

- What family values would you like to see reflected in your family's future giving?
- Are there areas of conflict within the family that must be acknowledged when developing a giving program?
- Do you want to bring future generations into the giving activities of your family?
- Has your family done any volunteering or giving together?
- What would be your vision for a collaborative giving effort within the family?

(g) Personal Values

- How and why have you settled on your life's work?

- What are the guiding principles that have helped you achieve in your business life? Personal life? Philanthropic life? Volunteer life?

- What is the best business decision you've ever made? How so?

- What is the best personal decision you've ever made? How so?

- If you could pass along a lesson to (your grandchildren/the people you help with your philanthropy/other organizations like us) what would that be?

- To what extent does our mission (vision, work) dovetail with your beliefs? How so?

- What do you expect from the charitable organizations in which you are involved?

- How do you like organizations to demonstrate their appreciation for gifts you have made?

- If I could demonstrate to you the true impact of your philanthropy, would you prefer: something named for you or someone you love; meeting some of the people you have helped; hearing from some of the people you have helped; receiving a report on how your money has been spent; all of the above?

(h) Follow-up questions

- How so?

- Can you clarify that?

- Can you give me an example of what you mean?

- What specific results are you looking for?

- Can you say more about that?

- Did I understand you correctly when you said...?

- How did that come about?

- What did that mean to you and your family?

- How strongly do you feel about that?

- What do you think about that?

- What is most important to you?

- Are we in agreement?

- Are you ready to move forward?

[These questions are adapted from "Asking Strategic Questions" by Karen Osborne, The Osborne Group, Inc., White Plains, NY. Used with permission.]

Model Standards of Practice for the Charitable Gift Planner

Preamble

The purpose of this statement is to encourage responsible gift planning by urging the adoption of the following Standards of Practice by all individuals who work in the charitable gift planning process, gift planning officers, fundraising consultants, attorneys, accountants, financial planners, life insurance agents and other financial services professionals (collectively referred to hereafter as "Gift Planners"), and by the institutions that these persons represent. This statement recognizes that the solicitation, planning, and administration of a charitable gift is a complex process involving philanthropic, personal, financial, and tax considerations, and often involves professionals from various disciplines whose goals should include working together to structure a gift that achieves a fair and proper balance between the interests of the donor and the purposes of the charitable institution.

I. Primacy of Philanthropic Motivation

The principal basis for making a charitable gift should be a desire on the part of the donor to support the work of charitable institutions.

II. Explanation of Tax Implications

Congress has provided tax incentives for charitable giving, and the emphasis in this statement on philanthropic motivation in no way minimizes the necessity and appropriateness of a full and accurate explanation by the Gift Planner of those incentives and their implications.

III. Full Disclosure

It is essential to the gift planning process that the role and relationships of all parties involved, including how and by whom each is compensated, be fully disclosed to the donor. A Gift Planner shall not act or purport to act as a representative of any charity without the express knowledge and approval of the charity, and shall not, while employed by the charity, act or purport to act as a representative of the donor, without the express consent of both the charity and the donor.

IV. Compensation

Compensation paid to Gift Planners shall be reasonable and proportionate to the services provided. Payment of finder's fees, commissions, or other fees by a donee organization to an independent Gift Planner as a condition for the delivery of a gift is never appropriate. Such payments lead to abusive practices and may violate certain state and federal regulations. Likewise, commission-based compensation for Gift Planners who are employed by a charitable institution is never appropriate.

V. Competence and Professionalism

The Gift Planner should strive to achieve and maintain a high degree of competence in his or her chosen area, and shall advise donors only in areas in which he or she is professionally qualified. It is a hallmark of professionalism for Gift Planners that they realize when they have reached the limits of their knowledge and expertise, and as a result, should include other professionals in the process. Such relationships should be characterized by courtesy, tact, and mutual respect.

VI. Consultation with Independent Advisers

A Gift Planner acting on behalf of a charity shall in all cases strongly encourage the donor to discuss the proposed gift with competent independent legal and tax advisers of the donor's choice.

VII. Consultation with Charities

Although Gift Planners frequently and properly counsel donors concerning specific charitable gifts without the prior knowledge or approval of the donee organization, the Gift Planner, in order to insure that the gift will accomplish the donor's objectives, should encourage the donor early in the gift planning process, to discuss the proposed gift with the charity to whom the gift is to be made. In cases where the donor desires anonymity, the Gift Planner shall endeavor, on behalf of the undisclosed donor, to obtain the charity's input in the gift planning process.

VIII. Description and Representation of Gift

The Gift Planner shall make every effort to assure that the donor receives a full description and an accurate representation of all aspects of any proposed charitable gift plan. The consequences for the charity, the donor, and, where applicable, the donor's family should be apparent, and the assumptions underlying any financial illustrations should be realistic.

IX. Full Compliance

A Gift Planner shall fully comply with and shall encourage other parties in the gift planning process to fully comply with both the letter and spirit of all applicable federal and state laws and regulations.

X. Public Trust

Gift Planners shall, in all dealings with donors, institutions, and other professionals, act with fairness, honesty, integrity, and openness. Except for compensation received for services, the terms of which have been disclosed to the donor, they shall have no vested interest that could result in personal gain.

Adopted and subscribed to by the National Committee on Planned Giving and the American Council on Gift Annuities, May 1991. Revised April 1999.

The Donor Bill of Rights

Philanthropy is based on voluntary action for the common good. It is a tradition of giving and sharing that is primary to the quality of life. To ensure that philanthropy merits the respect and trust of the general public, and that donors and prospective donors can have full confidence in the nonprofit organizations and causes they are asked to support, we declare that all donors have these rights:

1. To be informed of the organization's mission, of the way the organization intends to use donated resources, and of its capacity to use donations effectively for their intended purposes.

2. To be informed of the identity of those serving on the organization's governing board, and to expect the board to exercise prudent judgment in its stewardship responsibilities.

3. To have access to the organization's most recent financial statements.

4. To be assured their gifts will be used for the purposes for which they were given.

5. To receive appropriate acknowledgement and recognition.

6. To be assured that information about their donation is handled with respect and with confidentiality to the extent provided by law.

7. To expect that all relationships with individuals representing organizations of interest to the donor will be professional in nature.

8. To be informed whether those seeking donations are volunteers, employees of the organization, or hired solicitors.

9. To have the opportunity for their names to be deleted from mailing lists that an organization may intend to share.

10. To feel free to ask questions when making a donation and to receive prompt, truthful, and forthright answers.

> The Donor Bill of Rights was created by the American Association of Fund Raising Counsel (AAFRC), Association for Healthcare Philanthropy (AHP), the Association of Fundraising Professionals (AFP), and the Council for Advancement and Support of Education (CASE). It has been adopted by numerous organizations.
>
> Printed with permission of the Association of Fundraising Professionals.

Sample Acceptance Policies for Endowment Gifts

I. Purpose of Policies

The purpose of these policies is to provide a working document which serves as a guide for minimizing risk and maximizing the intended results of the organization's endowment building program. Specifically, it seeks:

- To support a program of asset development which encourages endowment gifts to further the organization's mission.

- To review opportunities for making planned gifts to permanently support the work of the organization.

- To clarify the terms of gifts which the Board authorizes the staff to accept on behalf of the organization.

- To educate the Board on potential problems that may make a particular gift unacceptable.

- To delineate the administrative responsibilities of the organization with respect to endowment gifts.

These policies do not embrace all areas in which judgment must be exercised. It is expected that additional policies and procedures will be added as appropriate.

The organization's management and administrative officers must exercise sound judgment in handling situations not specifically covered in these policies. In view of the importance of endowment gifts to the organization, those charged with attracting and maintaining them must be given wide latitude and, at the same time, must maintain the dignity and integrity of the organization and the best interests of its donors.

To that end, the organization subscribes to the *Model Standards of Practice for the Charitable Gift Planner* as adopted by the National Committee on Planned Giving and to the *Donor Bill of Rights* as created by the American Association of Fund Raising Counsel (AAFRC), Association for Healthcare Philanthropy (AHP), the Association of Fundraising Professionals (AFP), and the Council for Advancement and Support of Education (CASE). These codes for fundraising and planned giving practitioners are hereby incorporated as Appendix A of these policies.

II. General Statement of Policy

The organization has the responsibility to insure that any gifts it receives support its mission. Accordingly, the organization reserves the right to refuse any gift that it believes is not in the best interests of the organization and its constituents.

The organization also recognizes that the principle basis for making a charitable gift should be a desire on the part of the donor to support the work of the organization. No charitable gift, trust agreement, contract, or commitment may be urged upon any donor or prospective donor to benefit the organization at the expense of the donor's intent.

III. Types of Gifts

Various types of gifts may be contributed to the organization. Many are outright gifts by living donors, either on a one-time or a periodic basis. Others are deferred gifts that take effect upon the donor's death or at some future time. The organization receives the following types of gifts:

- Cash (including cash equivalents, such as Certificates of Deposit and savings accounts)

- Marketable securities (stocks, bonds, U.S. government securities)

- Closely held stock (non-publicly traded securities)
- Real estate
- Life insurance policies
- Other property (works of art, furniture/equipment, precious metals, etc.)

IV. Purposes of Gifts

Gifts of any size are welcome. Gifts may be given for current expenditures or for endowment, although these policies are directed toward endowment gifts.

(a) Named Funds

Named funds may be established with an endowment gift of $20,000 or more. In funds that are established with assets of $20,000 or more, distributions will begin after one year to allow the fund to earn income and provide realized and unrealized gain.

(b) General-Purpose Endowment Gifts

Many people choose to make unrestricted gifts to the organization's Endowment Fund. In such cases, the net assets released are used for ongoing operating expenses or selected priorities that the Board chooses.

(c) Donor-Designated Endowment Gifts

Others prefer to designate their gifts for one of the endowment's specific purpose funds:

- Communications and publications
- Scholarships
- Research
- Others

V. Acceptance of Gifts

(a) Gifts That the Executive Director May Accept

The Board of Directors has authorized the executive director to accept gifts for purposes consistent with the purposes and

203

Bylaws of the organization if such gifts are in the following forms:

- ○ Cash

- ○ Marketable securities

- ○ Tangible personal property valued at $500 or less

(b) Gifts Requiring Approval

Gifts requiring review and approval of the Board of Directors (or its authorized committee) include the following:

- ○ Gifts that have purposes that may fall outside the purposes and Bylaws of the organization

- ○ Life insurance

- ○ Closely held securities

- ○ Real estate

- ○ Other assets that may be unusual or fall outside the type of gifts usually handled by the organization

The organization shall seek legal and/or other professional counsel, as appropriate, in all matters pertaining to unusual gifts.

(c) Action to Accept Gifts

Contributions are recorded and deposited by the finance department within 24 hours of receipt unless special circumstances warrant further review of the gift. Gift acknowledgment letters are mailed within two business days of receipt of the gift.

Gifts that require review will be handled promptly by the staff calling a meeting of the Board of Directors and delivering all relevant information necessary to make a decision to Board members prior to the meeting. If a gift is not accepted, staff will notify the donor immediately. All gift reviews will be handled with confidentiality.

Special Notation: In certain instances (e.g., a gift on December 31), a decision regarding gift acceptance must be made immediately. In such a case, the staff will contact all members of the Board of Directors immediately. If not all members can be reached, approval to accept the gift can be made by either the Chair of the Board of Directors or the Chair of the Planned Giving Committee if there is concurrence with staff that the gift should be accepted without reservation. In the unlikely circumstance that neither of the above individuals can be reached, the executive director is authorized to accept such a gift if in his or her judgment there are no significant reservations. The executive director will report all such action to the Board of Directors.

(d) Gift Review Factors

Factors to be considered by the executive director and the Board of Directors in their review include:

○ The charitable intent and ultimate benefit to the organization and its constituents

○ The nature of any restrictions

○ The permanency of the gift

○ The administrative costs of managing the gift asset

○ Potential for actual or perceived conflict of interest

○ Consistency with the mission, purposes, bylaws, and policies of the organization

VI. Disposition of Gifts

(a) All Gifts

It is the policy of the organization to convert all gifts to cash and reinvest that cash according to the organization's *Investment and Spending Policies*. If assets offered to the organization are illiquid and cannot readily be sold, acceptance of the gift may depend on whether, in the judgment of the Board of Directors, a buyer is likely to be found within a reasonable period of time.

If a donor requests that the organization retain specific assets, the Board of Directors must decide whether acceptance and retention of the specific assets serves the purposes of the organization.

(b) Planned Gifts

The Board of Directors will direct all unrestricted gifts received as a result of planned giving to the Endowment Fund. Planned gifts that are donor designated will be used in a manner consistent with the donor's restriction.

The Board of Directors, in keeping with the organization's *Investment and Spending Policies*, will allocate annual distributions from the Endowment Fund.

(c) Memorial Gifts

Unrestricted memorial gifts will be directed to the Endowment Fund.

VII. Gift Valuation

The organization shall follow existing laws and Internal Revenue Service regulations for the valuation of gifts. Donors of gifts of cash or cash equivalents will receive receipts that include the amount and date of the gift. Gifts such as stock, real estate, personal property, life insurance, etc. require specific methods of valuation for the protection of both the donor and the organization.

(a) Publicly Traded Stocks and Bonds are accepted at the fair market value as determined under Internal Revenue Service rules. They are acknowledged by receipt for the number of shares given and the value of the securities on the date of the gift.

1. The value of the gift is the median market price on the date of the gift multiplied by the number of shares. The median price is determined by adding the high and the low stock price and dividing by two. The date of the gift is the date when the donor made the gift (as opposed to when the organization received notification of it).

2. Once the gift value is determined, the development officer prepares an acknowledgement letter to the donor for signature by the executive director.

(b) Life Insurance Policies: If the organization is made the owner of a term insurance policy, a receipt without gift valuation which describes the policy will be issued to the donor. If an insurance policy has a cash value at the time of the gift, a receipt containing the policy descriptions and the amount of the policy interpolated terminal reserve as of the date of the gift will be issued to the donor. A receipt will be issued for the value of all gifts contributed by the donor to the organization for the purposes of paying the premiums.

(c) Stock in Closely-held Corporations, Real Estate, and Personal Property will be reviewed by the Board of Directors prior to acceptance. Receipt for such gifts will reflect description of the gift only, omitting valuation. In instances where the organization issues a receipt with no financial valuation, the donor is required to establish the gift's value by independent appraisal. It is the donor's personal responsibility to defend against challenges to claims for tax benefits.

VIII. Gift Processing

(a) Contributions: Definition

Contributions are gifts of cash or other assets for which nothing of substantial value to the contributor is expected in return. These *Acceptance Policies for Endowment Gifts* cover contributions received through one of the planned giving vehicles described in Section IX.

(b) Gift Acknowledgement

Thank-you letters are prepared and sent to all contributors within two working days of receipt of the gift. The executive director signs acknowledgment letters to endowment donors. All such letters serve as a contribution receipt for the donor. Each letter will state *either* that no goods or services were received by the contributor in exchange for the gift *or* that goods and services were received by the contributor having a value of $_____.

The notice of a bequest will be directed to the executive director. A letter of condolence, signed by the executive director, will be sent immediately to the appropriate family member(s).

The development officer will request a copy of the will, any codicils, and any petitions from the attorney. He or she will also check the organization's files to determine if the donor, at some earlier time, sent a copy of the will or the wording of the provision to the organization. An expectancy file will be created in the donor's name.

(c) Donor Recognition

The organization realizes the paramount role of donors and their gifts in achieving its charitable purposes. Staff and Board members recognize donors in appropriate ways both publicly and privately, subject to the confidentiality provisions in Section XIII and the anonymous gifts provisions in Section VIII (d).

(d) Anonymous Gifts

A contributor's request to be anonymous will be honored and so noted in the contributor's file. If the name and address of the contributor is known, an acknowledgment letter will be sent which references the donor's request of anonymity.

IX. Planned Gifts

(a) Bequests

Bequests received by the organization will be applied to the charitable purposes requested by the donor. If no restrictions are specified, the Board of Directors will add the bequest assets to the Endowment Fund. Bequests of $20,000 or more establish a permanent named fund in the donor's memory. The staff will keep a file of expected bequests and will work with donors to insure that gifts intended to create a new fund meet with the organization's purposes and its capacity to carry out the donor's wishes.

(b) Charitable Remainder Unitrusts, Charitable Remainder Annuity Trusts, and Charitable Lead Trusts

The organization is an appropriate beneficiary of a charitable remainder unitrust (CRUT), charitable remainder annuity trust (CRAT), or charitable lead trust (CLT). The donor engages an independent trustee or serves as his or her own trustee; the organization does not serve as trustee. Because CRUTs, CRATs, and CLTs name the organization as beneficiary of the charitable interest, it is important that the staff work with the donor and the donor's counsel to insure that the organization will be able to carry out the donor's wishes. At the time of receipt of assets of $20,000 or more, a permanent named fund is established.

(c) Life Insurance

The donor may give an insurance policy outright to the organization. The donor names the organization as the owner and beneficiary of the life insurance policy and the organization retains the policy in its offices. Alternatively, the donor may decide to retain ownership of the policy and name the organization as the beneficiary. Upon redemption, a permanent endowed fund is established in the donor's name for gifts of $20,000 or more.

Premium payments may be made by the donor by direct payment to the organization at least 10 days prior to the premium due date. Such payments are deductible by the donor as charitable gifts for IRS income tax purposes. The organization cannot assume delinquent premium payments. In such instances, the policy will be canceled with the accrued cash value added to the organization's Endowment Fund in the donor's name. Premiums may be paid from accrued dividends or the accumulated cash value if the donor so stipulates only when such accrued dividends or accumulated cash value are sufficient to pay in full all remaining premiums.

(d) Charitable Gift Annuities

The organization may offer Charitable Gift Annuities through the local community foundation. The donor gives a gift of at least $10,000 to the community foundation for its Endowment Fund in the organization's name. The donor receives fixed and guaranteed income payments for the rest of his/her life and/or the life of a second person. Upon the donor's death (and that of the second person), the organization's Endowment Fund receives the unused portion of the gift. [Note that some community foundations charge a fee to administer Charitable Gift Annuities.]

The organization's development officer meets with the donor and community foundation's staff to complete the gift.

(e) Authority to Act on Behalf of the Organization

The executive director is authorized to represent the organization in facilitating charitable giving agreements with prospective donors and signs all such agreements on behalf of the organization.

X. The Organization's Legacy Society

The organization's Legacy Society is composed of individuals who have made plans to leave a gift to the organization through their estate plans. Every planned gift donor will automatically become a member of the Legacy Society. Members of the Legacy Society will be honored at appropriate special events and listed in the annual report

XI. Professional Advisors

The organization strongly encourages all donors to discuss proposed gifts with their legal and financial advisors. Prospective donors shall be advised, both orally and in writing, to seek their own counsel in matters related to charitable giving, tax, and estate planning. Likewise, the organization shall seek the advice of an experienced attorney when considering the acceptance of unusual or complex gifts.

XII. Publicity

No public media exposure with respect to his or her gift will be given any donor without the donor's consent. Donors will be asked to allow their "gift stories" to be told to encourage others to consider similar gifts.

XIII. Confidentiality

All information concerning donors and prospective donors, including names, names of beneficiaries, amount of gift, size of estate, etc. shall be kept strictly confidential by the organization and its authorized personnel unless permission is granted by the donor to release such information.

XIV. Review and Amendment of Policies

These Policies will be reviewed annually by the development (finance) committee and may be amended by the recommendation of the finance or development committee and approval by the Board of Trustees.

Sample Investment Policies Template

The < name > Community Foundation

Investment Policy Statement

PURPOSE

The purpose of this Investment Policy Statement is to establish a clear under-standing of the philosophy and the investment objectives for the <name> Community Foundation (hereinafter, the Foundation). This document will describe the standards that will be utilized by the Investment Committee in monitoring investment performance and will serve as a guideline for any investment manager retained.

The purpose of the Foundation is to accumulate a pool of assets sufficient to build community capital for future use with the corresponding obligation to support current and future community needs. These assets are to be invested in a manner consistent with statutory fiduciary responsibilities.

SCOPE

This Investment Policy Statement applies only to those assets for which the investment manager and the Investment Committee have discretionary authority.

INVESTMENT COMMITTEE

The Investment Committee is responsible for recommending investment policies and strategies, trustees, investment managers and/or advisors, and other fiduciaries, and monitoring the performance of the trustees, managers, advisors and other fiduciaries.

IMPLEMENTATION OF INVESTMENT POLICIES

The investment policies of the Foundation will be carried out by means of investment strategies that reflect continuous evaluation of changing investment environments, judgment regarding the allocation of the Foundation's assets among different kinds of investment opportunities, identification of appropriate investment vehicles, and the making of specific investment decisions.

STANDARD OF INVESTMENT JUDGMENT

In seeking to attain the investment objectives set forth in this statement, the Investment Committee shall exercise prudence and appropriate care.

SPENDING POLICY

Income available for spending is determined by a total return system. The amount to be spent in the coming year is calculated each <December 31st> and is reviewed and approved by the Investment Committee annually. The calculation is as follows: A 12 quarter rolling average of the market value is determined. The amount to be spent will be 5% of that 12 quarter rolling average of the market value. The "income" that may be spent, as determined in this paragraph, may be drawn from both ordinary income earned (i.e., dividends, interest, rents, royalties, etc.) and appreciation, both earned and unearned. All income and appreciation not needed to meet spending needs is credited directly to the Foundation and invested in the investment pools.

INVESTMENT OBJECTIVES

The primary objective of the investments will be *to provide for long-term growth of principal and income without undue exposure to risk* to enable the Foundation to make grants on a continuing and reasonably consistent basis. Therefore, the focus will be on consistent long-term capital appreciation, with income generation as a secondary consideration. More specifically, the Investment Committee seeks returns during a full market cycle that are large enough to preserve and enhance the real, inflation adjusted purchasing power of the Foundation's assets, while also considering the current spending requirements. In pursuing this objective, the Investment Committee endeavors to achieve total returns that, over time, are better than the relevant market averages. The Investment Committee does not expect that in each and every year the investment objective referred to above will necessarily be achieved.

TIME HORIZON

Due to the inevitability of short-term market fluctuations, it is intended that the following Specific Performance objectives will be achieved by the investment manager(s) over a *5-year moving period*, net of investment management fees. Nevertheless, the Investment Committee reserves the right to evaluate and make any necessary changes regarding the investment manager over a shorter term using the criteria established in the Evaluation of Investment Managers section of this statement.

SPECIFIC PERFORMANCE OBJECTIVES

Total Foundation

1. The total return shall exceed the Consumer Price Index plus 5% to be determined (5% premium reflects the average spending policy).

2. The total return shall exceed a target Balanced Index composed of: 40% of the S&P 500 Index (Domestic Large Cap Equity), 15% of the Russell 2000 Index (Domestic Small Cap Equity), 15% of the Morgan Stanley Capital International Europe, Australia, Far East Index–"EAFE" (International Equity), and 30% of the LB Aggregate Bond Index (Fixed Income).

Equity Managers

3. The total return shall exceed the total return of the relevant equity benchmark: Domestic Large Cap–S&P 500 Index, Domestic Small Cap–Russell 2000 Index, International–EAFE Index.

4. The manager's return will be expected to rank above the median return of the appropriate Equity Manager Universe, and of managers with a similar style.

5. The manager will be expected to maintain a beta (volatility) no greater than 1.20 versus the relevant equity benchmark.

6. The risk-adjusted performance (alpha) is expected to be positive.

Fixed Income Managers

7. The total return shall exceed the total return of the LB Aggregate Bond Index.

8. The manager's return will be expected to rank above the median return of the Fixed Income Manager Universe.

9. The manager will be expected to maintain a duration no greater than $\pm$ 25% that of the LB Aggregate Bond Index.

EVALUATION OF INVESTMENT MANAGERS

The investment managers will be reviewed on an ongoing basis and evaluated upon the following additional criteria:

10. Ability to meet or exceed the performance objectives stated in this Investment Policy Statement.

11. Adherence to the philosophy and style, which were articulated to the Investment Committee at, or subsequent to, the time the investment manager was retained.

12. Ability to meet or exceed the performance of other investment managers who adhere to the same or similar style.

13. Continuity of personnel and practices at the firm.

The investment manager shall immediately notify the Investment Committee in writing of any material changes in its investment outlook, strategy, portfolio structure, ownership, or senior personnel.

ASSET ALLOCATION

Deliberate management of the asset mix among classes of investments available to the Foundation is both a necessary and desirable responsibility. In the allocation of assets, diversification of investments among asset classes that are not similarly affected by economic, political, or social developments is a highly desirable objective. The diversification does not necessarily depend upon the number of industries or companies in a portfolio or their particular location, but rather upon the broad nature of such investments and of the factors that may influence them.

In making asset allocation judgments, the Investment Committee is *not* expected to seek to time subtle changes in financial markets or make frequent or minor adjustments. Instead, the Investment Committee is expected to develop and adopt expressed guidelines for broad allocations on a long-term basis, in light of current and projected investment environments.

To insure broad diversification in the long-term investment portfolios among the major categories of investments, asset allocation, as a percent of the total market value of the total long-term portfolio, will be set with the following target percentage and within the following ranges:

Total Foundation Type of Securities	Target	Equity Manager Range	Range	Fixed Income Manager Range
Equities				
Domestic Large Cap	40%	30–50%	90–100%	0%
Domestic Small Cap	15%	10–20%	90–100%	0%
International	15%	10–20%	90–100%	0%
Fixed Income	30%	20–40%	0%	90–100%
Cash	–	–	0–10%	0–10%

INVESTMENT MANAGER REQUIREMENTS

14. In today's rapidly changing and complex financial world, no list or types of categories of investments can provide continuously adequate guidance for achieving the Investment Committee's investment objectives. Any such list is likely to be too inflexible to be suitable for the market environment in which investment decisions must be made. Therefore, it is the process by which investment strategies and decisions are developed, analyzed, adopted, implemented and monitored, and the overall manner in which investment risk is managed, which determines whether an appropriate standard of reasonableness, care, and prudence has been met for the Foundation's investments.

15. Although there are no strict guidelines that will be utilized in selecting investment managers, the Investment Committee will consider the length of time the firm has been in existence, its track record, fees, assets under management, and the amount of assets the Foundation already has invested with the firm.

16. The requirements stated below apply to investments in nonmutual and nonpooled funds, where the investment manager is able to construct a separate, discretionary account on behalf of the Foundation. Although the Investment Committee cannot dictate policy to pooled/mutual fund investment managers, the Investment Committee's intent is to select and retain only pooled/mutual funds with policies that are similar to this policy statement. All managers (pooled/mutual and separate), however, are expected to achieve the performance objectives.

17. Unless prior written approval is obtained from the Investment Committee to the contrary:
    a. Each investment manager must satisfy the performance objectives and asset allocation guidelines.
    b. Each investment manager shall have the full investment discretion with regard to market timing and security selection, consistent with this Investment Policy Statement.
    c. The investment managers shall be evaluated on a quarterly basis and should be prepared to meet with the Investment Committee at least annually.
    d. The investment managers shall handle the voting of proxies and tendering of shares in a manner that is in the best interest of the Foundation and consistent with the investment objectives contained herein.
    e. The investment managers shall not utilize derivative securities to increase the actual or potential risk posture of the portfolio. Subject to other provisions in this Investment Policy Statement, the use of primary derivatives, including, but not limited to, structured notes,* lower class tranches of collateralized mortgage obligations (CMOs),** principal only (PO) or interest only (IO) strips, inverse floating securities, futures contracts, options, short sales, margin trading and such other specialized investment activity is prohibited.

       Moreover, the investment managers are precluded from using derivatives to effect a leveraged portfolio structure (if options and futures are specifically approved by the Investment Committee, such positions must be offset in their entirety by corresponding cash or securities).

The Investment Committee must explicitly authorize the use of such derivative instruments, and shall consider certain criteria including, but not limited to, the following:

   i. Manager's proven expertise in such category.

   ii. Value added by engaging in derivatives.

   iii. Liquidity of instruments.

   iv. Actively traded by major exchanges (or for over-the-counter positions, executed with major dealers).

   v. Manager's internal procedures to evaluate derivatives, such as scenario and volatility analysis and duration constraints.

       ★ Permit investments in "conservative" structured notes, which are principal guaranteed, unleveraged, and of short to intermediate maturity.

       ★★ Lower class defined by Federal Financial Institutional Examination Council (FFIEC).

  f. There shall be no investments in nonmarketable securities, except for Rule 144a securities (with or without registration rights). Rule 144a securities shall not exceed 20% of a fixed income manager's portfolio.

  g. For diversification purposes, the equity portion of each investment manager's portfolio should have in excess of 20 positions.

  h. Each investment manager must assure that no position of any one issuer shall exceed 8% of the manager's portfolio at market value, with the exception of securities issued by the U.S. government and its agencies.

  i. Each investment manager must assure that no more than 25% of its portfolio is invested in any one industry sector, with the exception of securities issued by the U.S. government and its agencies.

  j. The investment manager shall not effect a purchase that would cause a position in the portfolio to exceed 5% of the issue outstanding at market value.

k. The bond portfolio must have an overall weighted average credit rating of "A" or better by Moody's and Standard & Poor's rating services. In addition, there shall be no bond investments below investment grade (Baa/BBB). In the event that a bond instrument is downgraded below investment grade, then the investment manager shall immediately notify the Investment Committee in writing. In the case of a split rating, the higher rating will apply.

l. Not more than $500,000 of an investment manager's portfolio shall be invested in commercial paper of any one issuer. The credit quality must A1/P1.

m. Not more than $100,000 shall be invested in Bank Certificates of Deposit of any single issuer.

CONCLUSION

This statement of investment policy shall be reviewed annually. The investment performance will be reviewed on a quarterly basis and the report will be provided by an independent third party. The manager may provide any suggestions regarding appropriate adjustments to this statement or the manner in which investment performance is reviewed.

_____   _____

Acknowledged on behalf of   Date
\<NAME\> Community Foundation

_____   _____

Acknowledged on behalf of the   Date
Investment Manager

Reprinted with permission of the Council on Foundations

From the Community Foundations Leadership Team Best Practices, October 2002

Glossary of Endowment Terms

501(c)(3): Section of the Internal Revenue Code that delineates charitable and tax exempt status for an organization. Organizations qualifying under this section include religious, educational, charitable, amateur athletic, scientific or literary groups, organizations testing for public safety, or organizations involved in the prevention of cruelty to children or animals.

Accrual basis of accounting: An accounting method by which revenue is recorded in the period in which it is earned, regardless of when it is received. Likewise, expenses are recorded in the period in which they are incurred. Thus, earnings and expenses are recognized as services are rendered or consumed rather than when cash is received or paid.

Acknowledgment letter: A written expression of gratitude for a contribution sent by the organization to the donor that complies with IRS requirements for the type of gift received.

Agency endowment fund: A fund established at a community foundation by a nonprofit organization (agency) for the benefit of the nonprofit agency. The agency will receive a distribution periodically from the fund, determined by the foundation's endowment distribution policy. Also called *organization endowment fund*.

Annual giving program: A program that seeks gifts on an annual basis from its constituency; the income is generally used for operating budget support.

Anonymous gift: A gift that is not publicly attributed to the donor.

Appreciated assets: Assets that have increased in value since they were acquired.

Asset: Any thing of value including tangible personal property (collections, art, antiques), intangible personal property (stock and bonds, copyrights, patents), and real property (residence, vacation home, farm).

Asset allocation: For investment purposes, the distribution of the investment portfolio among various asset classes, including, but not limited to, domestic and foreign bonds, cash, real estate, venture capital, etc.

Bargain sale: The sale of securities, real estate, tangible personal property, or other assets to a charitable organization for less than their fair market value.

Bequest: A gift by will or trust. A charitable bequest is a gift by will or trust to a charity.

Capital campaign: An organized drive to raise substantial funds to finance major needs of an organization in a specified time frame.

Case for support: A written statement of the reasons why an organization merits financial support, including a statement of its mission, resources, potential for greater services, and future plans.

Case statement: A written statement, developed from the case for support, that presents the organization's mission, vision, and goals as persuasively as possible and is the foundation for marketing, promotion, cultivation, and solicitation efforts.

Cash basis of accounting: The accounting method by which revenue is recorded in the period when received and expenses are recorded in the period in which payment is made.

Cash gift: The most common type of gift made to charitable organizations, whether made by cash, check, and credit card.

Charitable deduction: The deduction taken on an income, gift, or estate tax return, federal or state, for the value of a gift made to a qualified charitable organization.

Charitable gift annuity: A gift made in exchange for the promise of lifetime income, immediate (CGA) or deferred (DCGA). It is a contract between the donor and charity that is part charitable gift and part purchase of an annuity. The total assets of the charity back its contract obligations.

Charitable lead trust: A charitable lead trust (CLT) pays the trust income to a charity for a specified period, with the principal reverting to the donor or another person(s) at the end of that period. If it is established by will, it is known as a testamentary charitable lead trust (TCLT).

Charitable remainder trust: A charitable remainder trust pays income to one or more beneficiaries for their lifetimes, a fixed term of not more than 20 years, or a combination of the two. When the trust term ends, the trust remainder passes to the charity. Charitable remainder trusts can be established as a charitable remainder annuity trust (CRAT) with a fixed payout or as a charitable remainder unitrust (CRUT) with a variable payout. They can be established during the donor's lifetime (CRT) or by the donor's will (TCRT).

Community Foundation: A tax-exempt, nonprofit, autonomous, publicly supported, nonsectarian philanthropic institution with a long-term goal of building permanent, named component funds established by many separate donors for the broad-based charitable benefit of the residents of a defined geographic area, typically no larger than a state.

Constituency: People who have a reason to relate to or care about an organization. These people typically fall into groupings such as faculty, staff, alumni, patrons, members, students, parents, and donors.

Consultant: A person with specific skills and experience who provides professional advice or services for a fee.

Custodian: A bank or other financial institution that has custody of assets that belong to an individual, corporation, or nonprofit organization. Custodians hold assets in safekeeping, collect income on securities in custody, settle transactions, invest cash overnight, handle corporate accounting, provide accounting reports, and other like services.

Cy Pres Doctrine: A legal doctrine from a French term meaning "as close as possible." When a charitable gift is made by will or trust and it is not possible to follow the instructions of the donor, a judge, estate, or trustee may apply the Cy Pres Doctrine to make the gift to an organization that comes closest to fulfilling the donor's wishes. It is usually applied when the named recipient of the gift does not exist, has dissolved, or no longer conducts the activity for which the gift is made.

Deferred gift: See *planned gift*.

Diversification: For investment management, an attempt to minimize risk by distributing assets among various asset classes or among managers within the same asset class who have different investment styles.

Dividend: A distribution of cash or securities by a corporation to its stockholders.

Donor: The individual or corporation that makes a charitable gift to a nonprofit organization.

Donor services: A planned program of development services to donors, their professional advisors, and their family members.

Endowment: An endowment is a pool of money that is invested to provide income and revenue for the nonprofit organization's operations or for a specific program. The Uniform Management of Institutional Funds Act (UMIFA) defines an endowment fund as "an institutional fund, or any part thereof, not wholly expendable on a current basis under the terms of the donor's gift agreement." The Financial Accounting Standards Board (FASB) has identified three types of endowments: (1) true endowment (in which the donor has stated that the gift is to be held permanently as an endowment), (2) quasi endowment (in which the organization's board of directors has designated organizational funds to the endowment, and (3) term endowment (in which the endowment is established for a set period of years or until a future event).

Endowment Action Program: An organization's written mission, case for support, objectives, strategy, and tactics to generate gifts to and growth of its endowment.

Fiduciary duty: The legal responsibility to act in the best interest of another party. For the boards of nonprofit organizations, such responsibility must be exercised on behalf of the organization in accordance with its governing documents.

Financial Accounting Standards Board (FASB): The board that issues Statements of Financial Accounting Standards that represent authoritative expressions of generally accepted accounting principles.

Financial statement: An accounting statement that describes the assets and liabilities of an individual or an entity, and its income and expenses. It quantitatively describes the financial health of the organization.

Form 990: The IRS Form filed annually by public charities. The IRS reviews Form 990 to assess compliance with the Internal Revenue Code. The Form lists the organization's assets, receipts, expenditures, and compensation of officers.

Fund: An account established for the purpose of tracking resources used for specific activities or objectives in accordance with applicable regulations, restrictions, or limitations.

Future interest: The right to receive property, whether real or personal, at some time in the future, either upon the occurrence of an event or upon a specified date.

Generally Accepted Accounting Principles (GAAP): The accounting standards and concepts used in the preparation of financial statements.

Gift, charitable: A gift is a transfer of property, whether real or personal, by one person to another without compensation. A charitable gift is a gift to a qualified organization for charitable purposes for which the donor does not reasonably anticipate benefit from the donee in return. IRC Section 170 and numerous court cases further define charitable gift.

Gift, historical value: The value of a charitable gift at the time it is given.

Gift, real value: The value of a charitable gift after adjustment for inflation and appreciation since the gift was made.

Income, earned: The interest and dividends made from an investment. See *return, rate of*.

Intangible personal property: An asset that has value but is not a physical object, such as stocks and bonds, copyrights, franchises, and trademarks.

Internal Revenue Service (IRS): The federal agency that regulates charitable organizations and their activities.

Legacy society: A recognition group established by the organization for donors who have made gifts to the organization through their wills or estate plans.

Life insurance (as wealth replacement): The use of life insurance to replace the value of an asset that has been donated to charity by paying the insurance premium with the tax savings resulting from the charitable deduction for the gift.

Life insurance (gift of): The irrevocable assignment of a life insurance policy to an organization for which the present value of the policy is tax-deductible.

Matching gift: A gift made with the specification that other gifts must be secured, either one-for-one or according to some other prescribed formula. Such gifts are usually required within a specified time period, with the objective of stimulating gifts from others.

Matching gifts program: A grant or contributions program that will match gifts made to charitable organizations. Each matching gift program establishes specific guidelines for the match.

Operating contribution: A contribution given to cover an organization's day-to-day, ongoing expenses, such as salaries, utilities, office supplies, and so on. Also referred to as *operating support*.

Operating support: See *operating contribution*.

Organization endowment fund: See *agency endowment fund*.

Personal property: Movable property, as distinguished from real estate (real property). See *asset, intangible personal property,* and *tangible personal property*.

Philanthropy: The word is of Greek origin, meaning love for humankind. Today, philanthropy includes the concept of voluntary giving by individuals or groups to promote the common good. Philanthropy includes voluntary service, voluntary association, and voluntary giving.

Planned gift: A gift in any amount and for any purpose that is carefully considered by the donor in light of estate or financial plans. It generally involves a staff person, a qualified volunteer, or the donor's legal and financial advisors.

Planned giving: The application of sound personal, financial, and estate planning concepts to the donor's plans for lifetime and testamentary giving.

Pledge: A promise to make future gifts to an organization. Some donors make multiyear pledges promising to give a specific amount of money each year.

Pooled income fund: A fund that receives gifts from multiple donors who, in return, receive life income interests based on the amount of their gifts to the fund and on the income earned by the fund. The principal of the fund is paid to the charitable organization at the death of the donor/beneficiary.

Public charity: A nonprofit organization that is exempt from federal income tax under Section 501(c)(3) of the Internal Revenue Code and that receives its financial support from a broad segment of the general public is a public charity for federal income tax purposes. Many organizations exempt under Section 501(c)(3) must pass a public support test to be considered public charities, or must be formed to benefit an organization that is a public charity. Charitable organizations that are not public charities are private foundations and are subject to more stringent regulatory and reporting requirements.

Real estate: Land and buildings thereon, home (residence or vacation), farm. Also known as *real property*.

Real property: See *real estate*.

Realized gains/losses: Increases/decreases in investments attributable to the sale of investments.

Restricted funds: Assets or income that is restricted in its use, in the types of organizations that may receive distributions from it, or in the procedures used to make distributions from such funds.

Retained life estate: The retention by the donor of the right to use and possess property for the donor's life, with use and possession transferring to the charity upon the death of the donor. See *future interest*.

Retirement plan assets: Assets held in qualified retirement plans including employers' pension or profit-sharing plans or salary deferral plans such as IRA, 401(k), and 403(b).

Return, rate of: The rate of return on an asset is a measure of investment performance and should be determined on a total-return basis (i.e., including realized and unrealized changes in market value in addition to earned income—dividend and interest income). Managers may report returns before or after management advisory fees, but returns are always reported after brokerage and trading costs.

Return, real: The real return is the nominal or actual return adjusted for inflation as measured by the Consumer Price Index (CPI).

Return, total: A measure of an investment's growth that includes both realized and unrealized changes in market value plus earned income. See *income, earned*.

Securities, closely held: Stocks and bonds of companies that are not traded on public exchanges; these companies are often owned by family members or by a few individuals. Also referred to as *securities, privately held*.

Securities (gift of): Gifts of securities include stocks, mutual funds, treasury bills, notes, and closely held stock.

Securities, privately held: See *securities, closely held*.

Securities, publicly traded: Stocks and bonds of companies that are traded on public exchanges.

Special event: A fundraising function designed to attract and involve people for the purpose of raising money or cultivating future donors.

Special gifts campaign: An effort to raise funds for specific purposes.

Spending policy: A organizational policy that states the percentage of a group of assets, such as an endowment, that should be distributed to support operations or programs.

Split interest gifts: Gifts that have two distinct parts or "interests": a charitable interest and a noncharitable interest. Also see *charitable gift annuity; charitable lead trust; charitable remainder trust; future interest; retained life estate.*

Stocks and bonds: See *securities (gift of).*

Supporting organization: A charity that is not required to meet the public support test because it supports a public charity. To be a supporting organization, a charity must meet one of three complex legal tests that assure, at a minimum, that the organization being supported has some influence over the actions of the supporting organization.

Tangible personal property: Coins, cars, books, jewelry, paintings, and other personal property you can touch. It does not include real property or intangible personal property.

Tax-exempt organizations: Organizations that do not have to pay state and/or federal income taxes. Federal tax-exempt status can be obtained by applying to the IRS, and in most states, for state income tax exemptions, to the state attorney general's office.

Unrealized gains/losses: Increases/decreases in investments attributable to the fluctuations in value of the investments from one time period to another.

Will: A written instrument by which a person makes disposition of his or her estate to take effect at death.

References

Ashton, Debra. *The Complete Guide to Planned Giving: Everything You Need to Know to Compete Successfully for Major Gifts*, Revised Third Edition. Quincy, MA: Ashton Associates, 2004.

Burnett, Ken. *Relationship Fundraising.* San Francisco: Jossey-Bass, 2002.

Ciconte, Barbara L. and Jeanne G. Jacob. *Fundraising Basics: A Complete Guide*, 2nd Edition, Gaithersburg, MD: Aspen Publishers, 2001.

Conway, Daniel. "Practicing Stewardship." *Hank Rosso's Achieving Excellence in Fund Raising*, 2nd Edition, Eugene R. Tempel, editor. San Francisco, CA: Jossey-Bass, 2003.

"Endowments." *The Chronicle of Higher Education and The Chronicle of Philanthropy.* Washington, D.C., May 27–28, 2004.

Gallagher, Janne G. "Legal Briefs." *Foundation News and Commentary.* Volume 44, No. 2, March/April, 2003. Washington, DC: Council on Foundations.

Jordan, Ronald and Katelyn Quynn. *Planned Giving: Management, Marketing and the Law.* New York: John Wiley & Sons, Inc., 2000.

Lord, James G. *The Raising of Money.* Cleveland, OH: Third Sector Press, 1983.

Moerschbaecher, Lynda S., with contributing authors Barbara G. Hammerman and James C. Soft. *Building an Endowment Right from the Start*. Chicago, IL: Precept Press, 2001.

Mourning, Steven L., "What Development Officers Need to Know About Investment Performance." *The Journal of Gift Planning*, National Committee on Planned Giving, Indianapolis, Indiana, 3rd Quarter, 2004.

National Conference of Commissioners on Uniform State Laws, "Uniform Management of Institutional Funds Act," 1972.

Newman, Diana S. *Opening Doors: Pathways to Diverse Donors*. San Francisco: Jossey-Bass, 2002.

"Planned Giving in the United States 2000: A Survey of Donors." National Committee on Planned Giving, 2001.

Robinson, Andy. *Selling Social Change (Without Selling Out)*. San Francisco: Jossey-Bass, 2002.

Schervish, Paul. *Major Donors, Major Motives: The People and Purposes Behind Major Gifts.* Boston: Social Welfare Research Institute, Boston College, 1997.

Stanley, Thomas J. and William D. Danko. *The Millionaire Next Door*. Atlanta, GA: Longstreet Press, 1996.

Wolfe, David B. with Robert E. Snyder. *Ageless Marketing*. Chicago, IL: Dearborn Trade Publishing, 2003.

Index